KNOW YOURSELF
AS A COACH

KNOW YOURSELF AS A COACH

DENNY KUIPER

iUniverse, Inc.
New York   Bloomington

Know Yourself as a Coach

iUniverse books may be ordered through booksellers or by contacting:

iUniverse
1663 Liberty Drive
Bloomington, IN 47403
www.iuniverse.com
1-800-Authors (1-800-288-4677)

ISBN: 978-0-595-52448-8 (pbk)
ISBN: 978-0-595-51647-6 (cloth)
ISBN: 978-0-595-62502-4 (ebk)

Printed in the United States of America

CONTENTS

PREFACE

Although I no longer play in organized athletics, I am an athlete. Although I am no longer at the helm of an athletic team, I am a coach. The terms "athlete" and "coach" help define who I am. Athletics has been an important part of my life since I was a young child. If you are reading this book, I am guessing it is or has been a way of life for you, too.

We athletes and coaches know the advantages of team participation, of learning and practicing and performing together, of reaching for the stars, even of failing. We know we are better for having made the effort.

My own experience led me into coaching basketball. Many of the examples I use in this book relate to basketball, but they can be applied to any sport at any level. My experience also led me into the counseling profession, which helped me look at working with young people differently than I had as a coach. That experience helped me better understand people and what motivates them. It made me a better coach.

I have observed and interacted with coaches and coaching staffs for a number of years, and I have learned much from those associations. This book is a compilation of my observations and experiences. The suggestions I offer are intended to help you improve your coaching skills and, perhaps, avoid some of the mistakes I have made. Most of all, I hope this book encourages you to think.

You probably will not agree with everything you read here. That is OK. Take from the book what you can. I *believe* everything I have written, but I am not so arrogant as to think that my way is the only way to coach. I do know I have included some valid points that coaches, typically, do not hear. Most coaches have not been trained or educated in those areas of human behavior. I am not suggesting that reading this book will make experts of coaches in those areas, but I believe the book is thought provoking and offers useful information that may help coaches improve.

What you won't find here is the normal coaching fare: the x's and o's of the sport, which plays to run in which situations. While strategizing is an exciting—and important—aspect of coaching, moving pieces around the field is only one element of coaching. Coaches are engaging people in play. This book focuses on how to engage people in play in ways that carry over into the rest of their lives.

I care very much about the coaching profession and the direction it is taking. This book is my contribution to the profession.

A WORD ABOUT THE USE OF MASCULINE PRONOUNS

I have used singular masculine pronouns throughout the book in a generic sense. That is, they are intended to represent a class of people whose gender is unknown or irrelevant. They also avoid the (to me) unwieldy use of "he or she," "himself or herself," and so on. The use of these pronouns should in no way be construed as exclusionary. Obviously, many fine athletes are females, as are many coaches.

ACKNOWLEDGMENTS

I want to extend sincere thanks to those of you with whom I worked, particularly, over the past few years. Many of the thoughts and ideas in this book come from conversations and interactions I have had with you: Neill Berry, Tim Buckley, Cypheus Bunton, Scott Cherry, Tom Crean, David Elson, Jon Harris, Scott Holsopple, Darrin Horn, Tod Kowalczyk, Steve Merfeld, Porter Moser, Dale Race, Mose Rison, Trey Schwab, Mark Simons, Dwayne Stephens, Jeff Strohm, and Brian Wardle.

Special thanks to Ralph Pim, Chip Pisoni, Dave Telep, Andi Seger, and Perk Weisenburger for their insights and observations. Thanks also to Anne R. Gibbons for her editorial assistance.

I owe an incredible debt of gratitude to my dear friend Carol Erickson for her part in helping me put my ideas together in a logical, concise, and understandable way. Carol, I could not have written this without you.

And, finally, I thank my daughters, Melissa and Amy, and my wife, Terree, for their love and support. Terree, your belief that I could write a book about coaching inspired me to do so. I appreciate your confidence in me and your encouragement when I needed it most. Much of what is written in this book I learned from you.

Of course, any errors that might have crept in to the book are my sole responsibility.

KNOW YOURSELF
AS A COACH

1ST QUARTER:

EXAMINE YOURSELF AS A COACH

1

WHAT IS COACHING?

In my travels as a consultant to college athletics, I hear repeatedly from coaches, "At this level, we can all coach." Then they go on to say, "Success is all about getting players." I think these statements are quite far from the truth. The disparity in the capabilities of one coach versus another, at times, is quite significant and does impact the success of teams beyond getting players.

When coaches make these statements, and quite frankly, those who do are usually young coaches, they mean they can diagram and draw up plays, watch film, and recognize offenses and defenses. While those skills are part of good coaching, there is much more to it than that.

Quite often when a coach is named to a coaching position, the first thing he does is to look at the team roster: the strengths, weaknesses, and what is lacking. High school coaches look at who is back for the upcoming year and what underclassmen show potential. College coaches look at what high school seniors are still available in the recruiting process and which younger players show promise. They jump into recruiting with both feet and full of vigor. Unfortunately, those coaches may be putting the cart before the horse. They need to shift their focus from others to themselves.

You, too, might better serve yourself and your program by taking time to examine some important issues. Before you look

3

outward at personnel, you might better look inward at your own motivation and how you envision the program and its function. Chapter 2, "Why Do You Coach?" will help you examine your motivation. It is time to set your course. Think beyond simply replicating the system under which you participated as an athlete or assistant coach. Ideally, you will have given this much thought and consideration during your assistant coaching years and have a good idea as to how you envision your program. But some inner reflection can be helpful after you get a new job, as well. Seeking out someone you can bounce ideas off of, someone who will provide encouragement and challenge, who respects you can be beneficial. Chapter 3, "Coaching Mentors," may be helpful in considering an appropriate person for that role. Looking inward with the support of a good mentor can help give you a sense of direction and understanding of your program.

You are like an architect, a person with the vision, the inspiration, and the design that you must communicate to those who will build it. You also serve as project manager, the one who oversees development and who assigns the tasks that will bring your design to completion. Your assistants are there to ensure that those tasks are accomplished efficiently. Being clear about those roles is essential to a quality program. Chapter 4, "Assistant Coaches," should help define those parameters and responsibilities.

As coach, you will determine the climate of your program. By climate, I mean the general "feel" of the program. Is it tense, changeable, consistent? Are rules communicated and followed? Is instruction clear? Do coaches and athletes demonstrate respect for one another? Because you determine the climate, you will want to know in advance what that will be. Chapters 5 through 12 will help you recognize what kind of climate you create and the best way for you to promote that climate.

Once you are clear about the climate you want, it is important for you to share verbally and behaviorally that information on a comprehensive and consistent basis with players, assistant coaches, and support staff. Chapters 13 through 15 address how to do this.

The road to having to a successful team is not always smooth. There will be tense situations that you will have to address. The recommendations in chapters 16 through 18 become more understandable and easier to implement when you are clear about who you are as a person and what you are trying to put into place.

You will have to determine what coaching styles you will use and what methods you are going to use to communicate that information to players and staff. Chapters 19 through 22 will help you accomplish that.

Next, you must get your team to buy in and be ready to play. How do you do that? Do you demonstrate a belief in your team? Does the team demonstrate belief in you and your staff? Chapters 23 through 25 speak to those topics.

After the vision and behavioral expectations have been established and communicated, you need to determine what the team will look like on the field or floor. What is the most effective way to play? What is the emphasis going to be? Will the team be forced into the coaching mold or will the coaching mold be fashioned to accentuate the team (its natural abilities and personality)? Chapters 26 through 30 will help you answer those questions.

Another important step is developing players—both physically and mentally. Since most coaches have spent a lot of time and focus on the physical development of players, this book does not address that issue. In chapters 31 through 36, however, I direct your attention to the mental development of your players. You need to be prepared to make decisions during the game to help to put your team in a position to win. When do you bunt? When do you go for it on fourth down? This book will help prepare you to be ready to make those decisions during the game.

Almost everyone agrees that coaching is much more involved than simply getting good players and putting them on the field or floor. It requires knowing who you are as a person and a coach, creating and sharing your vision, and enlisting the support of those in your program to model the behaviors necessary to realize that vision. Also, it requires selecting the best style of play to help your team be successful, developing your players not only physically but mentally, and being a good game coach. Coaching is challenging, to be sure. Hopefully, you will find information and encouragement in this book that will help you coach in a healthier and more consistent manner.

2

WHY DO YOU COACH?

If you read the preface, you have an idea of who I am, how I came to be a coach, and what prompted me to write this book. Equally important is who you are and what brings you to the coaching ranks.

Motivation plays a large part in determining how we approach our profession and how we relate to those with whom we interact in that profession. We coach in a manner that satisfies that motivation, whatever it is. If we are to be honest with ourselves and with others, we must know what it is that brings us to the coaching ranks. We must be able to answer the question Why do I coach?

To better understand what motivates us as coaches, we need to consider the answers to questions like these.

- What do I like about coaching?
- What do I dislike about coaching?
- How did I get into coaching?
- Who influenced me positively? Negatively?
- What does success mean to me? In life? On the playing field or court?
- What do I hope to accomplish?

Looking back, I had no clue why I wanted to be a coach other than that I loved playing. I knew I was not good enough to play beyond college; at the time, there seemed to be two choices for me: officiating or coaching. Since officiating did not appeal to me, I chose coaching. It allowed me to stay in the game.

Coaches get into the profession for various reasons. For some, coaching is a lifelong dream. They follow in the footsteps of someone they respect or who had a strong influence on them—a parent, a high school or college coach. For others a coaching job just seems to drop in their laps. Few enter coaching with a thorough understanding of the complexity and demands of the profession.

Perhaps the better question for those of us who have made coaching a profession is Why do I stay in coaching? The answer to that question might well provide us with better insight into our own coaching behaviors. The *way* we coach is in direct relationship to the *why* we coach.

Seldom do we act from a single motivation and seldom are all our motivations noble in nature. It is not my intent to judge the motivations or behaviors of coaches, but I do hope that you will recognize what it is that impels you to coach and understand the relationship between that impetus and the manner in which you coach.

Do you recognize yourself in any of the following descriptions?

1. You love the game. Whatever your sport, you are intrigued and fascinated by it. You love watching it and being a part of it. It is a significant element in your life.

   Potential outcomes:

   - Your love of the game inspires others to love the game as well.
   - The game consumes you, inhibiting a life outside of coaching.

2. You care about your players. You hope to have a positive impact on your players' lives.

   Potential outcomes:

   - Players are more interested in the fact you care about them than in what you know about your sport. (How do we know this? Read the comments of a recruit the next time he commits. Those comments are all about the coaches and the fact that the recruit believes the coaches care more about them as people than they do about the way they play defense.)

- You lose sight of the relationship boundaries with your players.
3. You see coaching as an opportunity to teach young people values and principles, as well as to share your knowledge of the game. You feel useful, and you serve an important function in their lives. Your goal is for your athletes to exhibit, on and off the court or playing field, the behaviors you have taught them and to do so with confidence, perseverance, and humility.

   Potential outcomes:
   - The positive influence you have on these players' lives compels them to extend that influence to others.
   - You attempt to force your value system onto your athletes.
4. You strive to develop relationships with the players in your program. When you work hard and sweat to achieve a common goal, a strong bond can develop between a player and a coach.

   Potential outcomes:
   - This relationship develops into a lifelong friendship.
   - Too often, I see and hear of players who, when they are done playing and when that relationship did not evolve, no longer want anything to do with their coach.
   - Sometimes, too, coaches will maintain relationships with only those athletes who go on to be successful (financially, athletically, or both).

     Example of an outcome: A few years ago, I ran into a parent of a player I once coached who told me that his son still talked about what a positive impact I had had on him. Of course, that made me feel good, but what made me feel especially good was the fact that this was a player who was not very skilled and who seldom played.
5. You like to win. It is why we keep score.

   Potential outcomes:

- You encourage a healthy competitive atmosphere, which is maintained fairly.
- Winning comes at the expense of everything else.

6. You love the adrenalin rush of competition. Nothing makes you feel more alive than being up or down a point or two with ten seconds to go in the game.

   Potential outcomes:
   - You coach well under pressure.
   - The rush excludes sound judgment and negatively impacts the outcome of the competition.

7. You enjoy attention and recognition.

   Potential outcomes:
   - You graciously receive appropriate recognition for a job well done.
   - You seek attention inappropriately, such as going out of your way on the sideline to be noticed or to appear on ESPN.

8. You coach to make money.

   Potential outcomes:
   - You receive an income consistent with others in your profession in similar situations to compensate you for a job well done.
   - Making more money becomes your primary objective, sometimes at the expense of the program and those people in it.

     Example of an outcome: I have heard professional and college coaches say, "I don't care if I get fired. I've got a five-year contract, and I am set for life." This attitude on the part of a coach pervades the entire program.

The motivations described above are representative of a host of others that contribute to a person's decision to coach or to remain in coaching. Each has its own potential outcomes, positive and negative. Each impacts the behavior of the coach and, thus, the entire program. If those motivations produce selfish outcomes (intended to promote oneself over the program) players and staff will have a difficult time believing in and supporting that coach and his approach.

Examine, for yourself, your reasons for coaching. Be honest. Look for the belief that lies behind the motivation. For example, if you are motivated by the need to win, ask yourself what you believe or have learned about losing. Does what you have learned still ring true? Have you learned something else to support or refute that? Do you need to change your thinking about the need to win?

If you discover that you have been operating from a false belief, that is, a belief that no longer serves you well, you might consider discussing it with someone you trust, someone whose judgment or experience offers insight. A mentor might serve this purpose.

Two things are certain: (1) Specific behaviors originate from specific beliefs and (2) those same behaviors produce the same results. Your success as a coach depends, in part, on how others perceive you, and that perception depends, in part, on how you behave. Whatever it is that brings you to coaching will be reflected in how you coach.

Dean Smith, the former basketball coach of the University of North Carolina, stands out for me as a man whose coaching motivation clearly was reflected in his coaching style: respectful and consistent. Those qualities earned him the admiration and respect of most people in his field. When you retire from the coaching profession, how will you be perceived?

3

COACHING MENTORS

In coaching, having a mentor—someone to share ideas with, seek advice from, and tap into his experience—is invaluable. Finding such a person may require time and thought.

Of course, our experiences in the athletic world go a long way in shaping us and the way we look at coaching. Most of us have been coached as athletes by a number of people. We have come in contact with many other coaches when we entered the coaching world. These people, potentially, can be mentors for us.

For the most part, I believe we function better if we take some time to determine whether or not we want a mentor and who that mentor should be. Sometimes, in our stubbornness and pride, we do not seek out anyone with whom to share ideas, or we use our high school or college coach or someone with whom we are familiar because it is easier. The relationship already exists; we don't have to work at developing it.

Relationships that evolve from specific roles, like coach and athlete, typically take on certain parameters/characteristics. When a person changes roles (athlete to coach, for example), he may stay "stuck" in the relationship as it was with that coach. Relationships between colleagues need to be based on equal footing. While one may have more experience hence, mentor status, that experience does not translate into more "power" or "control." The key in

11

mentor-mentee relationships, as I see it, is that they need to *develop* from a mutual respect and understanding. While the responsibility for developing that mutuality lies with both parties, the mentor has a unique opportunity to facilitate that growth by being willing to "give up" the pedestal position, thereby, empowering his mentee, which is, after all, the goal of mentor-mentee relationships.

So, could you benefit from a mentor? The quick answer seems to be yes. However, no mentor is better than a bad mentor. He has to be someone who helps you grow and develop as a coach. Also, if you become dependent and look to your mentor for the answers instead of suggestions, your development as a coach can be stunted. In general, the younger the coach, the more likely that having a mentor will be helpful. Mike Krzyzewski, the basketball coach at Duke University, said he always wanted an experienced, older coach on his staff. Then, one day, he did not need that any more. He had become the older, experienced coach. Though he may no longer have a mentor on staff, I suspect he has a person or two to whom he can reach out when needed.

The following are criteria to consider when deciding if you want a mentor and who that person should be.

1. What is your purpose in wanting a mentor? Many coaches will say they want somebody to tell them the truth; in reality, some do not.

2. Will your mentor tell you the truth even if you do not want to hear it? Will he challenge you to look inward to help you develop and evolve? Or will he just tell you what he thinks you want to hear?

3. What are your mentor's motives? Does the mentor really care about you and want you to become the best coach possible? Or does he want to be recognized? Is he self-serving?

4. Your mentor must know what you and your program stand for and what you are trying to accomplish. For example, if you believe in building your program with very athletic players, regardless of skill, and your potential mentor believes in building a program with skilled players, regardless of athletic ability, sharing ideas with him as to style of play would be counterproductive.

5. Is your mentor current? Is he keeping up with your team and your program? Is he available for you to get in contact with? With today's technology, it may not be necessary for him to live in your community, but he has to be accessible.

So, in summary, here are some questions to ask yourself as a coach.

- Do I have a mentor?
- If so, is my mentor effective, helping me and my team become better?
- If I do not have a mentor, do I feel the need for one?
- If I decide I want a mentor, am I willing to put in the time to select one who is best for me, not just one who is convenient?
- Am I willing to listen to my mentor, even if he has something negative to say?

Remember *The Godfather*? The don kept a consigliore around him to help him in sorting out possible options. A mentor doesn't need to be your best friend—indeed he shouldn't be. He just needs to meet the above criteria. Find a good mentor and you have an extra bonus for you and your program.

4

ASSISTANT COACHES

Being an assistant coach is a unique position. You have many of the same responsibilities and duties as the head coach, but not the same control and power. You come up with ideas and offer suggestions, but you make very few final decisions.

When starting out in the business as an assistant coach, it is important to find a program that fits you. Because jobs can be hard to come by, that may not always be possible. Nonetheless, during the application process, remember that while the program is interviewing you, you are also interviewing the program.

Ask yourself the following questions: Are my vision, goals, and way of doing things similar to those of the head coach? Is the head coach someone I respect and for whom I would enjoy working? Is the head coach a control freak? Does he micromanage? Will I be allowed to be myself? Is the head coach specific in defining my role? Will I be comfortable with my role? Is the coaching staff a group of people with whom I fit?

These are questions to ask yourself before accepting a job. Too frequently, I have heard coaches say, "I can work for anybody" only to leave the job a year or two later, because it was a "bad fit." A job interview is a two-way street. Ask questions during the interview process so you don't end up regretting your decision. Remember you can't back the head coach or sell a recruit if in the pit of your stomach the program doesn't feel right to you.

You should remember that you are on a team. You must learn how to be productive in that setting. You wear many hats and have myriad responsibilities, so you must be adept at working with a variety of people in different ways.

Occasionally, as an assistant coach you may be placed in awkward or difficult positions. You may not be certain what to do. Of course, your boss, the head coach, will impact significantly how you function, but understanding and accepting your role will help you form a basis from which to make hard decisions. The following guidelines may help you fully understand the role of assistant coach.

Cultivating Five Important Attributes

Keeping in mind the following five essentials will help you do a better job and help promote a smooth working relationship with the head coach.

1. *Loyalty.* You work for the head coach. Loyalty should be simple when it comes to such decisions as who plays, what style the team plays, and how practice is run because those are the head coach's decisions. Whether you agree or not, you need to be 100 percent dedicated to making the head coach's vision work. But at times the coach may make decisions with which you do not agree. Loyalty becomes much more difficult when the head coach operates contrary to your values and principles. Although there is no blueprint for how to deal with those types of situations, chapter 14 offers advice for your consideration when confronting loyalty issues.

2. *Vision.* What is the coach's vision for the program? What does the head coach want the program to look like? Once you understand that, determining how you should function and how to react to a given situation is easier.

3. *Operating style.* How does the head coach operate? Remember: You adjust to him; he does not adjust to you.

15

4. *Ownership.* It is your program too. You are part of it. Your name is linked with it. When your team wins, you win. When your team loses, you lose. By thinking and functioning as part of a team, you will be a bigger asset to the program and more ready for a head coaching position.

5. *Selling the program and the head coach.* Always remember you are representing the program and the head coach, not just yourself. In fact, your emphasis should be on the program and the head coach.

Achieving Effective Communications

Another important aspect of an assistant coach's job is communication. You will need to have meaningful communication about the program with a variety of people (e.g., the head coach, fellow assistant coaches, players, trainers, managers, academic advisors, facility managers). Making sure everyone understands what is happening is of the utmost importance.

1. *Timing.* A head coach's plate is almost always very full. Knowing when to bring an issue to his attention is important. Is it urgent or can it wait? Ask yourself: Is this the best time to talk to the boss about this or is it just more convenient for me? Young coaches laced with passion and energy (which are great traits) often rush headlong into the head coach's office. Before you do that, take a breath. What's important to you at the moment may in fact be just a drop in the vast ocean of what the head coach is dealing with. Of course, you should bring the really important stuff (anything that might embarrass the head coach or the program) to his attention as soon as possible.

2. *Staff interaction.* Do more than your share to develop pleasant relationships. Almost certainly you will get along with some staff members better than others. It is not okay just to say, I do not relate very well to so-and-so. Make an extra effort to cultivate an amiable working relationship with all your colleagues. Do not be the one who causes friction and tension on the staff.

3. *Relationships with players.* Get to know the players. Developing a relationship with them takes work. Be careful not to pick and choose, developing relationships only with players you like or those who readily buy into your methods. Be aware of the balancing act between being a confidant to a player while being loyal to the head coach and the program. You are not helping the kid or the program if you let him play you against the head coach.

4. *Empathy.* Try to understand and put yourself in the shoes of people you communicate with on a fairly frequent basis. By doing that you will better hear them and their concerns, which facilitates the communication process.

Being a Part of the Decision-Making

Even though as an assistant coach you do not usually make the final decision, you will often be involved in the decision-making process. It is important to become proficient in anticipating and planning for what the team and the program need.

1. *Think twice and study.* Suggestions for changes to the program are most helpful when they have been thought through and carefully studied. Unstudied options are just brainstorming. There is a time and place for that, but make sure you understand the difference between brainstorming and thought-out suggestions.

2. *Anticipate, anticipate.* What are we lacking? What can we do better? How can we better teach, recruit? Where are we going to be next week, next month, next year? What are we going to have to change? Be proactive, not reactive.

3. *Be a self-starter.* Being a self-starter is not only a sign of initiative, it's a marker for confidence. Be active within the confines of your program. What does that mean? Coming up with an idea for a 1-2-2 zone press is easy. Researching, getting tapes, and preparing to sell the head coach on why it would work is another story.

4. *Think like the head coach.* When uncertain what to do, ask yourself, what would the head coach want me to do, then use your perception and skills to respond accordingly.

5. *Apply the 25 percent rule.* Find your strengths as an assistant coach and go with them. Find your weaknesses and improve 25 percent. (See chapter 32 for a fuller discussion of this rule.)
6. *Present solutions—not problems.* The head coach wants help with answers. He does not need an assistant telling him we cannot stop the run, we are being out rebounded. He sees that; he wants to know how to fix it.

Achieving Emotional Stability

Work at being emotionally healthy. See if you are bringing your baggage to the table. If so, make an effort to eliminate or reduce it. The following suggestions may help you do that.

1. *Know your place.* It is always important to remember you are an assistant, an important role, but you are not the center of attention. You may be doing great things with players or with recruiting, but it is not your job to bring attention to yourself. Your head coach may do that for you, and your good work will be noticed. Your role as an assistant is to be part of the program.
2. *Avoid jealously.* Sometimes another assistant may be the one that comes up with a great idea or finds a great recruit. Be happy for him and the team. Avoid being the assistant coach that always needs to be noticed and given credit.
3. *Accept criticism.* Yes, at times you will be unfairly criticized by the head coach. Deal with it.

As an assistant coach, undoubtedly you will be placed in uncomfortable or comprising positions at times. Anticipating the unforeseen can reduce difficulties and consequences later. By better understanding your role, you can do a lot to prevent problems. Hopefully, the guidelines in this chapter will be of assistance.

2ND QUARTER:

EXAMINE YOURSELF AS A PERSON

5

WHAT DEFINES YOU?

When my daughters, Melissa and Amy, were in college, they told me that when they were younger they were always glad when the team I was coaching won on Friday night. Since neither was a very rabid sports fan and each had her own interests outside of my coaching life, I asked why. They told me that winning made for a more pleasant weekend—not exactly an endorsement of their father's ability to deal with losses.

For a coach, losing a game can feel very personal. We question what we did wrong and what we could have done differently. We allow the outcome of the game to determine the way we interact with family and friends. We may pout, mope, express anger, or in general, let the loss dictate the quality of life for us and those around us. In reality, we are the same coach when we lose as we are when we win. In fact, at times, we may coach a better game in a loss than in a victory. It is one game. To let it define how we view ourselves as a coach and determine how we behave toward others puts too much emphasis on the outcome of the game. That outcome does not determine who we are as people.

I remember my team losing a game on a last-second shot at the buzzer. Devastated, as many coaches are in that situation, I got into my car and drove, ending up ninety miles away in Flint, Michigan, where I went through a Burger King drive-through and drove back home. I allowed the loss to define me: I was a loser, as a coach and as a person. Needless to say, I had a miserable weekend, which affected my family and friends, as well as me.

In addition to defining themselves by wins and losses, many coaches define themselves by their title. They thrive in an environment where they are the center of attention, where conversation is about their profession, and where anything outside that realm seems a distraction. At all levels, coaches draw attention. Junior and senior high school coaches are well known around town; people ask them questions about their teams. College coaches, especially at the highest level, are very visible people; much attention comes their way. What coaches do is important. They teach young people many life skills. But what other people are doing is also important. Do not take yourself too seriously, and do try to cultivate the whole person rather than simply the coach.

The importance of this was brought home to me when, after seventeen years of coaching, I found myself out of a coaching position for one year. One Friday night in early December, while I was shopping in a mall, I remember thinking, "What are all of these people doing here? Don't they know there are high school games going on? Don't they care?" In truth most of them probably did not know and if they did, they did not care. I had been so immersed in the high school coaching arena for so many years, that I had a distorted perception of the importance of what I did as a coach.

One program with which I have had the privilege of working for the past six years is the basketball program of Wisconsin-Green Bay. Tod Kowalczyk, the head coach, has an excellent understanding of himself as a coach and as a person. Hard working, he puts tons of energy into his program. At the same time he sees himself as Tod—not Tod the Coach. He is a great husband, father, and friend. Wins feel great to him, and losses hurt, but they do not define him as a coach and person. Whenever possible, Tod spends Wednesday night at dinner with friends. I have attended three or four of those dinners and am amazed at the diversity of the people in attendance: politicians, sports administrators, small business owners, and professionals from other walks of life.

Sport is a topic of conversation, but it is one of many topics of conversation. Tod is one in a group. He is not Coach Kowalczyk; he is Tod. The conversation does not revolve around him. He not only is comfortable with that, he likes it.

What we do as coaches is important, to us, to those with whom we work, and to the fans who enjoy watching our sport, but it isn't the only show in town. Like Tod Kowalczyk, coaches need to broaden their sphere of interest, invest in relationships with people outside the field of sport, and in themselves, valuing the person as well as the coach.

6

ARE YOU HEALTHY?

You cannot be a successful coach for a long period of time unless you are healthy. Health, both physical and emotional, affects coaching performance. It is not uncommon for coaches to neglect their health, because, in their minds, they do not have the time for it. Working eighty to a hundred hours a week, they have too much to do. In reality, they cannot afford *not* to take the time to take care of themselves.

Over the past few years in particular, we've seen a number of extreme examples of coaches being suspended, fired, or quitting their jobs because of poor physical or emotional health. These are coaches with obesity problems, heart problems, drug and alcohol problems, sexual addictions, and gambling problems. Most likely, there are other coaches with comparable issues who just have not been exposed yet. Coaching is a stressful profession, and that stress is compounded when a coach ignores the impact it has on his professional and personal life. Unhealthy coaches lose patience, focus, and self-control, which then transfers to those around him—players, colleagues, friends, and family. They all deserve better.

Let's look first at physical well-being. Choosing to be physically healthy is a lifestyle commitment. It requires true diligence, especially as coaches work long hours, travel a lot, and stay up late at night, all of which makes it difficult to eat, sleep, and exercise on a regular basis. Coaches who keep going on caffeine can only do so for so long.

1. Sleep
   - Get the proper amount of rest each night.
   - When forced to function on a shortage of sleep, get back on track soon as possible.
2. Proper diet
   - Avoid fast foods.
   - Drink soda, alcohol, and coffee in moderation.
   - Drink plenty of water.
   - Eat plenty of fruits and vegetables.
3. Exercise
   - Work out forty-five to sixty minutes a day, four to five days a week.
   - Include stretching, aerobic, and muscle-toning exercises.
   - Work with a strength coach or trainer to help set up a proper program for you.

Emotional well-being is as important as physical well-being, but being physically fit goes a long way in supporting emotional health. If you are not caring for yourself physically, you are much more likely to be emotionally unfit.

Emotional issues surface in the coaching ranks frequently because the position is under such public scrutiny. That spotlight on a coach draws his most basic insecurities to the front. The objective for the coach, then, is to mask or subdue them, to reduce visibility.

What are some of the emotional issues that plague coaches?

- paranoia
- insecurity
- abuse of power/control (see chapters 8 and 9)
- a we versus them mentality
- addiction

Addictions of any type require total loyalty from the addict. Nothing will usurp their place in the life of an addict. Someone addicted to a particular substance or behavior will have a rough go of trying to meet the demands of coaching while maintaining that addiction. That is, of course, unless the addiction is coaching,

25

a variation on the addiction to work. Like workaholics in other arenas, workaholic coaches are praised for their seemingly selfless dedication of time and energy. Unlike the alcoholic or excessive gambler, the workaholic coach does not suffer the same kind of public condemnation for his addiction. Ironically, the praise those coaches receive serves only to feed the addiction.

Coaching can be a lonely job, especially for head coaches. That feeling of loneliness often evolves into a kind of insecurity, a paranoid delusion that everybody is against you. Coaches become distrustful and may resort to an "us against the world" mentality. A judicious amount of that mentality can be motivating, especially in road games, but too much of it compels the coach to demand total loyalty from his players and assistant coaches. He exacts this loyalty by exerting power and control over every person in and every aspect of the program.

I remember very clearly being in a locker room several years ago after a lopsided defeat when the head coach drew a big circle on the blackboard and told everyone that if they were "in," that is, committed to him, to write their name inside the circle. On the surface, it did not seem like such a bad idea. You cannot have success if assistant coaches or players can choose to be "in" or "out" at their convenience. However, it did not play out that way. In this case, the coach used the signatures to justify whatever actions he took. He held those signatures over people's heads and used them as leverage. The lesson being taught there was emotionally unhealthy; the players were taught to distrust everyone but the coach. They had to either endure the situation or buy into the rationalizations of the coach. The coach's insecurity, paranoia, and distrustfulness played out over the whole season.

Poor emotional health stems from negative beliefs. We can trace almost any negative interaction to the belief that produces it. Though we generally want to blame others for our bad feelings or behavior, in actuality the responsibility belongs to us. Coaches could reduce the incidence and intensity of unhealthy interactions among themselves and players if they understood and acted upon this premise.

For example, a player rolls his eyes when the coach tells him something. This happened to me at times when I was coaching. I am willing to bet it has happened to you. The coach's response or reaction is based on what he believes the player "meant" by his action (in this case, rolling the eyes). Typically, we interpret rolling the eyes to mean that the person believes we don't know what we are talking about or has a here-we-go-again attitude, neither of which seems very respectful. The coach may respond or react. If he responds, he names the offending behavior and the consequence of it. If he reacts, he allows the behavior to trigger the unhealthy belief that his authority has been threatened, and he may "go off" on the player. Some coaches go so far as to verbally abuse players for what may be fairly trivial issues. That is not to say that we should not confront those behaviors. Failure to confront disrespectful or inappropriate behavior contributes to an unsafe environment. Everyone in the program needs to know what the parameters of acceptable behavior are and that unacceptable behavior will not be tolerated.

Although typically not part of the coach's responsibility, helping athletes and others to understand what precipitates their own behavior will help the program succeed. If coaches encourage their players to recognize what they tell themselves when their emotions are triggered (when they are ready to explode in reaction to something someone did or said), they may be able to rewrite that message and respond differently.

Going back to the player who rolled his eyes, consider what may have been the player's internal message that resulted in that behavior in the first place. The coach sternly tells the player that his position on a particular play was incorrect. The player rolls his eyes. Why? There may be any number of reasons, none of which were intended as a challenge to the coach's authority. Perhaps the tone of voice the coach used reminded the player of a parent's or previous coach's repeated scolding, which triggered the thought "I can never get it right." The player's reaction may have been more about his history with a parent or a previous coach than about the current coach. For the coach's part, if he believes categorically that he deserves respect, the disrespectful behavior of another will not threaten him. He will need to address it, but it won't trigger inappropriate behavior on his part. Looking back at my coaching career, there were times I addressed the behaviors inappropriately because at that particular time I was not emotionally healthy.

If you make emotional health a goal, you likely will exhibit the following behavioral characteristics:

- You deal with situations in a mature, adult manner.
- You do not have vices that impede your ability to coach your team in an effective way.
- Your relationships are not toxic.
- Whatever issues you may have are addressed in a productive way (therapy, self-help, etc.) and do not carry over to your team.

I recently asked the father of a coach if he ever gave his son any coaching advice. "Only that to be really successful," he said, "you must have inner peace and serenity. If you do not, it will affect you and your coaching success." How profound. There is a quote in the fitness center I work out in that speaks to inner peace and serenity: "Begin your day with five minutes of quiet introspective, sit still, close your eyes, and relax. Focus on your breathing and let the world become simple and peaceful."

The best example a coach can give his athletes is that of a healthy individual, one who strives for balance in his life and who respects the same needs in others. Healthy people create healthy programs. Healthy programs nurture the people who function within them.

Ask yourself as a coach "Would I want to play for me? Am I the type of coach who inspires players, teaches life lessons, and models healthy behavior?"

Becoming physically and emotionally healthy is a process, a process that requires the same kind of diligence and self-discipline familiar to athletes in training.. But while the benefits of sports training last only so long as the athlete plays that sport, the benefits of being physically and emotionally healthy last a lifetime.

7

WHAT IS YOUR MOTIVATION?

As a coach you are in a position of power and control. You make decisions that affect the lives of people on your team. For that reason, it is important to understand the motivation that influences those decisions.

One way you can recognize what it is that motivates you is to look at who benefits or whose needs are met by the decisions you make. If a decision you make does not benefit a team member or the team as a whole or is otherwise unproductive, then it isn't a sound decision to make. In fact, it may be counterproductive and cause difficulties later.

I clearly recall a time following a tough Tuesday night loss, when I, as a high school coach, decided to have a very intense, physical, going-back-to-the-fundamentals practice on Wednesday and Thursday in preparation for Friday night's game. The practices on Wednesday and Thursday were terrific. However, we lost again on Friday to a team we should have beaten. We were beaten on Tuesday because we were unprepared to attack a zone defense. The same thing happened again on Friday. What the team needed was a better understanding of and practice against a zone defense. Instead, I decided to focus on trying to upgrade the intensity and desire. The players responded well, but that was not the problem. Looking back, I recognize that my motivation was selfish. I was feeling down about Tuesday's loss and the Wednesday and Thursday practices were to make myself feel better.

I once had a college coach call me following a game to tell me that his team had won but that he had really chewed out his team and staff after the game. When I asked him why, he said the game had been frustrating and he was feeling frustrated and angry. When I asked him if he thought his team and staff deserved the chewing out and whether it helped them, he admitted it had not. He was frustrated and his purpose was to express that frustration so he could feel better.

I am not suggesting that you cannot have tough practices or call out members of the program. Of course, you can. At times that is the best course of action. The key is to know why it is being done: Is it to improve play or to improve the program? Or, is it to meet your needs?

As a coach you are not always going to act from unselfish motives. You are human. What you can do is recognize your motivation, understand why that motivation influences your responses, and do your best to ensure that your responses are appropriate.

Some things to consider that will help you recognize your motivations:

- What triggers your thoughts and feelings? Where are you internally? Are you responding to what is actually going on or to what the event triggers in you?
- Whose needs are being met? Are you considering your players' needs, the team's needs, the program's needs, or only your own needs? Seeking temporary solutions to meet your own needs may feel good at the time but may lead to potential relationship problems later.
- Where does your frustration belong? It is unfair to take out your frustration on undeserving people just because you can. Yelling at your team because you are frustrated with the bus driver who took a wrong turn on the way to the game is inappropriate.

Below are some questions to ask yourself concerning motivation:

- Am I willing to examine my motivation in my coaching decisions?
- Do I believe my motivation should be to do what is best for the team?
- If my motivation is selfish, am I willing to attempt to change?

8

POWER

Being in charge is an awesome responsibility. As a coach, you have responsibility for any number of people. It really does not matter at what level you coach—junior high through the professional ranks—being in charge is being in charge, and being in charge means having power.

Somewhere along the line, I heard the statement "power corrupts; absolute power corrupts absolutely." It is said, too, that the true test of a person's character is not only how he deals with adversity, but also with how he deals with power. The abuse of power forces others to try to cope in a harmful environment and can have long-term and far-reaching impact.

History is full of people in and out of the sports arena who have misused power, but coaches, especially those who work with children and young adults, have the potential to cause severe harm by abusing that power.

How do you know when you abuse the power you have? Taking a look at the following points is a good start in determining whether you abuse power.

- Do you recognize your own attitudes and biases? You have preconceptions based on your own experiences. Do you view power as a right of the position? Are you getting your needs met by exercising that power?

- Have you studied appropriate ways to exercise power? K-12 educators take between one and one and a half years of coursework, as well as student teaching, before being given control of a classroom. They are taught how to work with young people and how to use their power in a positive manner. Many college and professional coaches do not get that training. Their degrees may be in chemistry, business, accounting, etc., with no training in education, whatsoever. Being properly trained does not guarantee you will use your power well, but it does help you understand the dynamics of personal development.
- Do you operate and use power like your previous boss or mentor? Often, young assistant coaches who have been treated poorly or abusively emulate that behavior with others when they become head coaches.
- Are you held accountable? If you are in a position where the administrator, the athletic director, or both are unaware of what goes on in the program or do not hold you accountable, you are more vulnerable to abusing power. Who holds you accountable if your chain of command does not?

To be a coach who chooses to wield power in a productive way, the following steps are suggested:

1. Make a decision to use power in a healthy manner. If in doubt as to what is healthy, err on the side of caution. For those coaches who have not had good examples of using power in a healthy manner, this will be more difficult to do.
2. Take a course, program, or workshop on being the person in charge. Talk with other coaches who are not seen as power abusers.
3. Examine your attitudes toward power and try to determine if you have abusive traits. Ask people you trust—both those you have worked for and those who have worked for you—to be honest with you about whether you exhibit abusive traits.
4. Do not emulate the manner of handling power exhibited by former coaches or those for whom you have worked. They

may or may not have used power appropriately. Find your own way.

5. Hold yourself accountable for using power appropriately. Find a boss, friend, someone on your staff who will tell you the truth regarding how you use power.

6. Evaluate your team-program needs. Try to meet those needs rather than your own.

If you are a coach who has abused power, making a change will not be easy. There is a reason you have abused power. Maybe you have needs that are not being met, or maybe you simply do not know how to use power in a healthy manner. You will have to examine your situation and determine what needs are being fulfilled by an abuse of power and whether you are willing to change. You might have to get out of your comfort zone and acknowledge you have not seen healthy use of power, so you do not how to do that. But the first step, a willingness to want to coach without abusing power, is a great start and will help create an environment that is safer and more enjoyable for everyone involved in the program.

It *is* possible to have power and wield it well. We do not have to look any further than coaches like Tony Dungy, the head coach of the very successful Indianapolis Colts. Coaches and players, alike, praise him as a great coach and one who exerts power in a healthy manner.

9

CONTROL

There is an old saying, "Those in control do not always have to have control." Having control of a team or program does not mean you have to do everything or micromanage. The type of team you coach determines how much may be delegated to assistant coaches, support staff, and others. If you are a head football coach in college or the professional ranks, you obviously cannot do it all. You must allow position coaches to coach. If you are the cross-country coach at the high school level, you probably have to do most, if not all, of the coaching and support work. No matter whether you are the head coach, an assistant coach, a support staff person, you have some degree of control. Typically, the greater the title, the greater degree of control you are given—and the more vigilant you need to be to ensure you use it appropriately.

I suspect a number of coaches confuse control with respect. They think if they are running everything, looking over people's shoulders, they have control and everybody recognizes that and respects them. I do not believe that is the case. Being in control means you are willing to let others contribute. Of course, you monitor what your staff is teaching and doing, but you do that with the intent of helping them to improve, not with the idea that you will take over. If you try to do everything yourself, a lot of peoplepower is going to waste. Ask yourself the following questions to help you understand that.

1. Can I allow members of my staff or team to be in roles of leadership when it is for the betterment of the team?
2. Can I allow an assistant to teach drills, do scouting reports, and help make game plans?
3. Are players allowed to be open in making comments and suggestions in team meetings, practices, and games?
4. Is an environment created during discussions where members of the program feel comfortable in voicing their opinions, without fear of being put down? Is the environment round table or top down?
5. If I feel insecure, do I let everybody know I am in charge by lowering the hammer and asserting my authority?
6. Do I care who gets the credit? If a member of the program is particularly adept at teaching a certain aspect of the game or relates well to a particular player, do I allow that person to use those skills?
7. Have I ever commented to the media about the role a particular assistant played in the development of strategy or the game plan? When he coached at Illinois, Bill Self gave assistants television assignments before games to share in the experiences of a head coach. Do I do that for my assistants?

Having everybody acting like a productive member of the program is a shining example of a coach truly being in charge. Keep your finger on the pulse of the situation but your hands out of everybody's pockets. Empowering your staff will not only help them grow, it will foster trust in and commitment to the program.

10

RESPECT

Respect is as essential in the coaching world as it is in any other profession. We want respect and we value it. We like the feeling we get when we believe someone respects us. Conversely, when someone disrespects us, it feels lousy. Like good communication and trust, respect must be mutually shared to be real. If we are in a position of some power, we may receive a semblance of respect because of that position or title, but neither ensures real respect. Basically, we have little, if any, control over whether people respect us.

- You cannot force someone to respect you.
- When a person does not show you respect, it says more about that person than it does about you.
- If you believe you deserve respect, you will not buy into another's lack of respect toward you.

I suspect disrespect toward others begins with a disrespect of self. Most of our rude, dismissive, and otherwise abusive behavior comes from a lack of our own sense of self-worth. Similar to bullying, disrespectful behavior provides us with a false sense of control. We use it to "even the score," so to speak, to make up for being discounted or the feeling that we have been discounted. We need to recognize our own inclination toward disrespect.

How can we identify our own potential for exhibiting disrespect?

- Explore instances when you have been inclined to react to what you interpreted as disrespectful behavior toward you.
- Were your reactions immediate or did you consider what your response would be?
- What feeling or feelings were present at that moment?
- What did you tell yourself about the behavior and the individual exhibiting the behavior?

Once you have analyzed your internal messages, the meaning you give to the incident, you are ready to confront it appropriately.

- Confront the person by telling him the behavior you observed and that it was inconsistent with your expectations.
- Reinforce the behavior you do expect.
- Ask the individual whether he has anything to say regarding the behavior.
- Listen and respond (being mindful that your response is not reactive, i.e., provoked).

Frequently, I have heard coaches say, "Why would I show respect to someone when I do not respect him?" The answer is he is a fellow human being. There is a big difference between respecting someone and showing someone respect. An example is a player you may have on your team who has little discipline, is rude, lazy, unfriendly, distant, and not very coachable. You may not respect him or his behaviors. You don't need to. You also do not have to compromise yourself. You can and should address his inappropriate behaviors, but if you do that in a disrespectful way, you will have little impact on his behavior. You will be exhibiting the same disrespectful behavior that he exhibits toward you

How do we respectfully approach everyone, even the most disrespectful?

1. Value each individual as a person of significance.
2. Understand that everyone has feelings that are conflicted at times, especially under pressure, and that those feelings,

and the beliefs that precipitate them, give rise to behavior that sometimes is inappropriate.

3. Live by the golden rule: Do unto others as you would have them do unto you. Your own behavior as a coach goes a long way in modeling the kind of behavior you desire and expect from your athletes and staff:

- Be on time. When you are late and make people wait, just because you can, you communicate to them that your time is more important than theirs. If something comes up, causing you to be late, apologize for your tardiness.
- Avoid sarcasm. It is demeaning.
- Avoid name-calling. It is degrading.
- Avoid the silent treatment. To ignore a player or another coach dismisses them as a person. Show enough class to address issues that need addressing, rather than resorting to mind games.
- Allow people to be who they are: They do not have to live life according to your standards or rules. They do, however, need to be held accountable for team standards and rules.

It is important to understand that showing respect is a daily necessity. You do not get to pick and choose when and to whom you want to show respect. If you would like others to show you respect, you need to model the behavior. You need to show respect to everyone—media, managers, officials, fans, and so on, not just people in positions of power.

Looking back at my coaching career I did not always show respect. I regret that. I could rationalize away or otherwise justify my behavior by saying: He was a poor coach. That player was soft. The official was awful. The media asked a really stupid question. But the reality is I had and still have a choice to show respect to people or not.

As a coach, whether you like it or not, you are modeling behavior for the players on your team. What message do you want to communicate when it comes to showing respect?

When I think of a coach who is humble and treats all people, not just the "important" people, with respect, I think of Jerry Moore, football coach of three-time defending NCAA Division 1 Football Championship Subdivision (formerly 1AA) National Champions Appalachian State. My stepson, Jeff Yardley, played for Appalachian State in the late 1990s. Jeff began as a walk-on and later became a scholarship player. He speaks very highly of Coach Moore and the manner in which he treated and respected his players throughout Jeff's career there. Coach Moore sends a powerful message. What message do you send?

11

INTEGRITY

Barry Bonds is indicted by the grand jury for lying about using steroids. Kelvin Sampson, basketball coach, makes hundreds of phone calls in violation of NCAA rules while at Oklahoma University and Indiana University and loses his job at Indiana. Marion Jones forfeits her gold medals from Olympic events because of steroid use. New England Patriots coach Bill Belichick, in an incident now known as Spygate, is fined five hundred thousand dollars by the NFL for using illegal video taping. George O'Leary loses his job as football coach at Notre Dame because of an inaccurate résumé. Michael Vick is sent to prison for two years because of his involvement with dog fighting. A powerful high school football program in Alabama has come under attack for numerous violations, not the least of which is an administrator who forces teachers to change grades so athletes will be eligible. These are just some of the more unsavory stories that have occurred in the past few years in athletics.

The question one cannot help but ask is where is the integrity in athletics? Of course, for every story we hear about that involves cheating or illegal activity, there are many we do not hear about of coaches and athletes who abide by and operate within the rules, but the influence of unethical activity and downright cheating that occurs in athletics is impossible to ignore. And indeed we should not ignore it.

It seems to me that most coaches go into the profession with noble intentions and, then, over a period of time, gradually step over the line more and more when it comes to operating in an honest way. Coaches have told me that what we do is minor compared to what school X does when it comes to following the rules, as if to say metaphorically shoplifting isn't as bad as armed robbery. Others have said their compliance officer is good; he isn't always checking out every little thing. While still others say their compliance officer is not very good; he always wants to check it out to see if it is allowable. Too often, I see coaches and athletes rationalizing away their integrity: "I only bend (or break) the little rules." "Everybody else does it too." How did we get to this point?

Athletes and coaches, naturally, are highly competitive, and they participate in a very competitive environment. Several factors related to that competitiveness contribute to the cheating and unsavory approach used by some coaches and athletes.

- **Money, money, money**
  The amount of money made by
  coaches in major football and
  basketball programs is huge. Many
  make as much as four to five times
  more than the presidents of their
  universities. Professional athletes
  and coaches are in another world all
  together. They want to win to keep
  their jobs and continue to make the
  big money.

- **Pressure to win**
  Having job security and producing
  a winning program are two
  powerful motivators for coaches
  who struggle to win, especially
  when other coaches and programs
  are not operating within the rules.
  That inequity gives rise to the belief

that they must bend the rules in order to compete.

- **Looking for the edge**
  Coaches and athletes look for the little things that will help them get over the top. They want to win, sometimes at any cost.

- **Purpose**
  They forgot their purpose, the reasons they coach. (See chapter 2, "Why Do You Coach?")

- **Choosing not to know**
  Some coaches will say, "I did not know my assistant was doing that; I cannot be responsible for everything going on in the program."

- **Supporting the coaching fraternity**
  Coaches sometimes choose to stick up for other coaches when they get in trouble for cheating or unethical behavior, proving to that person they are a good friend. They will say, "I know he has done some shaky things, but he has always treated me well." America is a country of giving people second, sometimes third or even fourth, chances. But when someone cheats and another coach goes out of his way to help save that person from the resultant penalty, he contributes to the problem.

As a coach, you often work in a vacuum. You associate and interact with other people in the world of athletics, often isolated from the real world. Behavior that some people would never consider accepting or doing becomes a norm for some coaches. Without realizing it, perhaps, you gradually step over the line and rationalize away your integrity. When you compromise your integrity, you surrender your dignity.

I believe a large majority of coaches want to coach in the most ethical and honest way. At times they get sidetracked. It will take a conscious commitment by you to run your program and team with integrity.

12

TIME-STRESS

Coaches, from recreation leagues to the professional ranks, assume a great many responsibilities and feel, at times, overwhelmed by the demands upon their time and attention. Every person in a program has expectations of the coach. Those expectations, in total, are unrealistic, and the coach who tries to meet them all will wear himself out in the attempt. It isn't only the expectations of others that create tension for a coach; his own expectations may be inappropriate or distorted.

In order to examine the suitability of those expectations, a coach needs to begin with a value's check. The exercise below, developed by Susan Pearce for a Student Assistance Training Guidebook, will help facilitate that. This may be done alone or in a group (with assistant coaches, perhaps). The initial brainstorming may be a group activity, but different people probably will have different responses when it comes to prioritizing values.

Step 1. Brainstorm and list areas of value to you.

- family
- job
- church
- recreation
- health
- continue list as needed...

Step 2. Take a sheet of white 8½ by 11 paper and let it represent the totality of those things you value. Rip it into pieces so the size of each piece is consistent with how much you value each item on your list. Write the corresponding value on each piece of the paper.

- family (might be the largest piece)
- job (might be the next largest piece)
- health (might be the third largest piece)
- and so on from there . . .

Step 3. Stack the pieces of white paper and set them aside.

Step 4. Take a sheet of colored paper (the same size as the white paper) and let it represent the totality of the time you have. Look back at your initial values list (not the pieces of white paper) and rip the colored paper into pieces to represent the amount of time you spend on each value area. Write that value on that piece of paper.

- Which value area takes up the most time?
- Which value area takes up the next most time?
- And so on . . .
- Continue until you've used up all your paper (time) and included all your values.

Step 5. Now, match up the corresponding values from the white and the colored paper pieces. Take note of any incongruence in paper size.

The intent of this exercise is to point out that for most of us (perhaps coaches, in particular), there will be a disparity between what we believe our values to be and the amount of time we actually spend cultivating those values. It is that incongruence that causes stress in our lives. If our values and the way we use our time (or the way we function) are in conflict, we will be conflicted or stressed.

Becoming less stressed is not about finding the newest time-management device or better ways to multitask. It is about living the life we value. We need to walk our talk, and our talk needs to be real.

It has taken me some time to realize in what way my own values influence how I choose to spend my time and how I would want to coach. Perhaps life's lessons have taught me that a winning record does not translate into a winning person, that the most important aspect of coaching, for me, is developing relationships with my players—relationships that afford me the opportunity to encourage, teach, and support them in realizing their full potential as people and as athletes.

Understanding my own value system, then, helps clarify why I respond as I do to certain coaching behaviors in others. A few years ago, I worked with a coaching staff that stated repeatedly that they wished they had more time to spend and talk with the athlete outside the athletic arena. What can be more important for a coach than to give some of his time to a player? Prioritizing time is of utmost importance. Learning to say no sometimes is necessary.

About three years ago, I received the following e-mail. The author is unknown (though various people have been given credit for it). In any case, the story speaks poignantly to the issue of values.

A young man learns what's most important in life from the guy next door.

It had been some time since Jack had seen the old man. College, girls, career, and life itself got in the way. In fact, Jack moved clear across the country in pursuit of his dreams.

There, in the rush of his busy life, Jack had little time to think about the past and often no time to spend with those important to him. He was working on his future, and nothing could stop him.

Over the phone, his mother told him, "Mr. Belser died last night. The funeral is Wednesday." Memories flashed through his mind like an old newsreel as he sat quietly remembering his childhood days.

"Jack, did you hear me?"

"Oh, sorry, Mom, Yes, I heard you. It's been so long since I thought of him. I'm sorry, but I honestly thought he died years ago," Jack said.

"Well, he did not forget you. Every time I saw him he'd ask how you were doing. He'd reminisce about the many days you spent over on 'his side of the fence' as he put it," Mom told him.

"I loved that old house he lived in," Jack said.

"You know, Jack, after your father died, Mr. Belser stepped in to make sure you had a man's influence in your life," he said.

"He's the one who taught me carpentry," Jack responded. "I wouldn't be in this business if it weren't for him. He spent a lot of time teaching me things he thought were important. Mom, I'll be there for the funeral," Jack said.

As busy as he was, he kept his word. Jack caught the next flight to his hometown. Mr. Belser's funeral was small and uneventful. He had no children of his own, and most of his relatives had passed away. The night before Jack had to return home, he and his Mom stopped by to see the old house next door one more time. Standing in the doorway, Jack paused for a moment. It was like crossing over into another dimension, a leap through time and space. The house was exactly as he remembered. Every step held memories. Every picture, every piece of furniture . . . Jack stopped suddenly.

"What's wrong, Jack?" his Mom asked.

"The box is gone," he said.

"What box?"

"There was a small gold box that he kept locked on top of his desk. I must have asked him a thousand times what was inside. All he'd ever tell me was 'the thing I value most.'" Jack said.

It was gone. Everything about the house was exactly how Jack remembered it, except for the box. He figured someone from the Belser family had taken it.

"Now I'll never know what was so valuable to him," Jack said. "I guess I'd better get some sleep; I have an early flight home, Mom."

It had been about two weeks since Mr. Belser died. Returning home from work one day, Jack discovered a note in his mailbox. "Signature required on a package. No one home for delivery. Please pick up at the main post office within the next three days," the note read.

Early the next day, Jack retrieved the package. The small box was old and looked like it had been mailed a hundred years ago. The handwriting was difficult to read but the return address caught his attention. It read, "Harold Belser."

Jack took the box out to his car and ripped open the package. There, inside, was the gold box and an envelope. Jack's hands shook as he read the note inside: "Upon my death, please forward this box and its contents to Jack Bennett. It's the thing I valued most in my life." A small key was taped to the letter. His heart racing, as tears filled his eyes, Jack carefully unlocked the box. There, inside, he found a beautiful gold pocket watch. Running his fingers slowly over the finely etched casing, he unlatched the cover. Inside he found these words engraved: "Jack, Thanks for your time! Harold Belser."

"The thing he valued most... was... my time." Jack held the watch for a few minutes, then called his office and cleared his appointments for the next two days.

"Why?" Janet, his assistant, asked.

"I need to spend some time with my son," he said. "Oh, and Janet... thanks for your time!"

Life is not measured by the number of breaths we take but by the moments that take our breath away.

3RD QUARTER:

PUT YOUR PEOPLE SKILLS TO WORK IN COACHING

13

LISTEN AND OBSERVE

Unfortunately, listening and observing are two skills that coaches, and, indeed, people in general, have not developed or utilized well. Why is that? First, I suspect, a good number of coaches are unaware of the absence of those skills in their repertoire of coaching tactics. In order to improve a skill, one, first, must be aware of the need for it.

Second, coaches function in leadership roles. Often, leaders, either from a sense of necessity or a natural propensity, do a lot of talking—informing, analyzing, instructing, directing—from positions of authority. They may do this to impress people or to convince others of the legitimacy of their positions, or they may sincerely believe that they are providing the leadership needed to improve the program. In either case, a coach who neglects to listen and observe diminishes the capacity of his team to develop. When we listen to and observe our players and our coaching staff, we see the program evolve.

Third, we fail to listen and observe because we may not like what we learn. We may neglect to ask questions, or if we do ask questions, we phrase them in a way that will ensure the answer we want to hear. For example, we have a particular play we want our players and coaches to support. We may ask them, "What do you think of play A?" which gives them the opportunity to answer honestly. The more likely question will be worded as, "Play A is great, isn't it?" To the latter question our players and coaches know the answer for which we are looking. We think we are seeking their input; they know otherwise.

If you commit to improving your listening and observation skills, you will become a better coach, enhance your communication, and develop better relationships with your colleagues and your players.

During the course of my coaching and consulting career, I have learned a number of strategies that are helpful in improving listening skills.

- Ask open-ended questions, such has, "Tell me something about yourself that I do not know." "What types of things do you like to do in your spare time?" "What is most important to you in your life?" These questions do not encourage "yes" or "no" answers.
- Do not interrupt. Make it a point in your conversations to let the person finish his point. Use follow-up questions to let the person know you were listening to what he had to say.
- When someone relates an incident or event in his life, do not try to "top" it. In fact, it is best not to shift attention away from his story by relating your similar story unless it would be helpful to let him know you understand what he has experienced.
- When assistant coaches and fellow head coaches are speaking, make a conscious effort to listen and learn. You do not always have to summarize or clarify what they have said.

On one occasion when I was an assistant coach, the head coach told the team, "Without looking at the wall of the arena name the five companies whose advertisements appear on the wall." The most any player could recall was three. To be perfectly honest, three is all I could name, as well. This is an arena where the players and I worked every day for two to three hours. Our observation skills were not very good. The exercise made me wonder what else the players and I were missing.

Here's an idea you might want to try. Stop practice and ask each player and coach to describe what he sees from where he stands at the moment on the floor. Tell him to include not only what he sees but also what he makes of it (its meaning, as he sees it.). Is the play working? Is the right person getting the ball? How is the defense playing? What are the playing conditions? Is it hot or cold in the gym? Am I in good position to observe? Each person will have a "view" unique to himself based on the physical position he has on the floor or field and based on his perception of the practice or game and his participation in it. Even those on the bench will have a perception that contributes to the game, perhaps a broader perspective or one more attitudinal in nature.

Exercises like that can benefit the team.

- You are teaching your players and coaches how to observe.
- You demonstrate the value of each person's observation and participation.
- You help the team see the big picture and appreciate more what is happening on the whole floor or field instead of just a player's own part in it.

Teach yourself to be more observant, and to listen and make better choices based on the expanded information rather than relying on reactive choices based on your patterns of behavior. Encourage that behavior in your coaches and players.

14

COMMUNICATION, LOYALTY, TRUST, AND OWNERSHIP

Communication, loyalty, trust, and ownership are powerful words often used in the athletic world. But what do they mean and how do we cultivate them?

I believe loyalty, trust, and ownership can be developed and enhanced only through open, honest communication. For a coach to facilitate that communication, he must take the time not only to listen to athletes and staff—their ideas and concerns—but also to give those ideas and concerns real consideration. (See chapter 13, "Listen and Observe.") For communication to be effective, it must exist on a two-way street.

Effective communication should be discussed and modeled. One means of modeling that communication is for the coach to begin the season by talking to the team about who he is and how the team will operate. For example, he might tell the team he has experience working with teams and some solid ideas about how the game should be played and how the program should function. He might tell them, also, that he would like them to learn to trust that. In addition, he might explain the importance and process of communication in the program—how decisions will be made, problems solved, people's concerns aired. He needs to communicate expectations, as well. Players who know what is expected of them and the process to follow to get information or assistance will perform better on and off the court or field of play.

The head coach needs to operate similarly with his coaching staff, telling them what they can expect from him as head coach, including his position of authority, and what he expects from them. He might give them the opportunity to think about and share expectations of themselves and others within the latitude given by the head coach.

What meaning do you give loyalty in the athletic setting?

- Loyalty means being true to the program, which includes the way the game is played—the specific set of rules—and the coaches, staff, and teammates.
- Loyalty works in every direction. A coach needs to show loyalty to the people, staff, and athletes in the program. Too often, I suspect coaches expect and demand loyalty, but do not always give it in return.

Trust grows when you believe another's words, behaviors, and motives to be honest and when that belief is affirmed over time. As a coach you should only say what you mean; what you can back up. Too often coaches say or do something they do not mean or cannot back up. For example, they promise playing time, scholarships, and so on. They try to motivate players, psych them up, play head games with people, using dishonest or deceitful comments. When that happens and the coach's dishonesty is exposed, trust is broken. The work and time it takes to regain that trust is significant. I believe, however, more trust can be built when, on those occasions, a coach owns up to his error, apologizes, if necessary, restates his point or position appropriately, and moves on.

Trust on the floor and field is of utmost importance. Basically, what it means, is that an athlete is confident his teammate has his back, and is doing what he is supposed to be doing. For example in baseball, if the coach gives the hit and run sign, the runner on first is running and trusts that his teammate at bat is going to swing at the pitch, no matter whether it is a ball or strike, and try to put the ball in play. In basketball, when a player double-teams the low post, he trusts that his teammate is going to rotate to his person, who was left open.

How do you encourage players to have ownership in the team and the program, to really feel that they and their ideas matter? You get players to that point by caring about them and their ideas. Players need to know that their opinions, feelings, and ideas do count. For example, you may try an idea that a player or the team really believes has merit, even if you don't think it will work. If you try it for a while and it does not work, the fact you "tried" and were willing to extend trust to the athlete and team will go a long way in building ownership in the team. Sometimes, those ideas may work, as in the case at Western Kentucky, a team I worked with during 2006 season. David Elson, the coach, and I had talked about the players developing more ownership in the team. Coach Elson let Justin Haddix, the quarterback, put in a couple of offensive plays. The plays proved to be very successful. That would never have happened if Coach Elson had not encouraged ownership.

It is not enough for you to say you need loyalty, trust, and ownership in your program. You need to model it and practice it. You, as the coach, have the final say, but when everyone believes that he is valued and counts, the commitment level rises.

15

LEADERSHIP

Repeatedly, through my travels as a consultant, I hear coaches lament, "Kids today don't have good leadership skills and those who exhibit some inclination for leadership don't know how to use the skills they have."

If that is the case, I would ask, "Why?" and "What can we do to change it?" I suspect the perception of those coaches is accurate. From my point of view in the athletic setting, young people do seem to show fewer leadership skills than young people did a good number of years ago. I believe the reasons for that are varied.

One of the reasons, I believe, lies with the adults and coaches rather than with the athletes. From Little League to summer camps, from junior high through college, adults organize sport. Coaches put players on teams, decide how the game will be played, and establish all of the rules Young people show less leadership skill today because, for the most part, they are not given much opportunity to develop those skills.

Before summer camps and AAU, young people organized their games on their own. Someone would step up and take charge, show leadership skills. When things did not work out, arguments arose, and the participants resolved them on their own. Kids learned to take responsibility.

If young people are going to learn leadership skills, we need to be intentional about providing the training. There are organizations, too numerous to mention, that have made leadership building a goal, but perhaps the most evident is the military academy system. It is virtually impossible to graduate from an academy without exhibiting leadership skills. The academies are constantly putting the cadets in positions of leadership and letting them experience success or failure based on their own experience and skills.

When you give young people the opportunity and skill-building necessary to develop leadership qualities it results in better-prepared leaders, in our classrooms and on the playing field. Those leaders will progress to board rooms, political arenas, classrooms, and hospitals. They will initiate charity drives and alumni organizations, programs for disadvantaged youth, and earth-keeping initiatives. In short, they will help create an environment that nurtures leadership skills in the generations to follow.

What can coaches do to contribute to that long-range goal as well as to the short-term goal of developing leadership on his team? Two perspectives emerge for me when I consider an answer to that question. First, I look at the coach as leader, and second, I look at how the coach may cultivate leadership on his team.

Coach as Leader

The position of coach is a leadership position, whether he perceives himself as such or not. He can be a positive or a negative leader. He can work toward becoming a more effective leader or do nothing and maintain whatever leadership skills he already may or may not possess. Good leaders are of sound character and exhibit traits that enhance the team. Below are a few of the traits I have observed while working with coaches and teams.

1. A good leader is unselfish. He gives the honor and credit to others. In that way, he builds confidence and trust.
2. A good leader criticizes the performance or behavior, not the person. When an individual is not performing up to standards, a good leader has the responsibility to hold that person accountable and confront the behavior. He must be fair, firm, and consistent in that effort. When that occurs, the

person learns to trust the leader's judgment and concern for him as a person.

3. A good leader walks his talk. What a leader does speaks louder than any number of words he utters. He may be extremely knowledgeable about his subject or profession, but if that knowledge isn't supported by action, it is worth little.

4. A good leader exercises authority. He commands rather than demands respect. Authority, appropriately and evenly applied, creates an environment of safety.

5. A good leader recognizes the way his emotions and behavior impact his team. Allowing his emotions full sway when inspiring and encouraging his team may be effective. Allowing his emotions full sway when he is angry or insecure is a dangerous way to operate.

Coach as Cultivator

Again, through observations and conversations with a number of coaches and players, I have some suggestions for coaches who want to cultivate leadership skills in their players.

1. Put members of your teams in positions where they must make decisions. Let them pick teams. Let them coach their team occasionally. Let them hammer out any problems.

2. Have players address the team. They can do some of the scouting reports. They can talk about what they feel the team needs to do to improve. They can challenge the team to dare to be great.

3. Give your staff and players responsibility. If they misuse or mishandle it, address it, but do not avoid giving them responsibility because you are afraid they won't handle it as well as you would. Do not micromanage. Give them a chance to grow.

4. Have team activities that require goal-setting without coaches in attendance.

5. Have team goals and objectives selected by the team.

6. Elect a team council that will meet weekly to address problems or to determine the state of the union (team).

7. Reinforce the fact that the team is made up of and belongs to everyone. No one person has more ownership (not to be confused with authority) than another.

As young people are provided the opportunities and the resources to develop leadership skills, they will utilize them. You need to trust them in that process. Trust is the greatest gift you can offer them.

16

CONFRONTATION

Confrontation occurs in coaching. Unfortunately, the very idea of confrontation provokes feelings of unease for a number of people. Depending on our experience with confrontation, the way or ways it was modeled for us as we grew, we have developed patterns of behavior upon which we rely when confrontation surfaces. They may or may not be particularly healthy behavior patterns.

For some, any hint of confrontation means a threat, so the reaction is one typical of a threat response: fight or flight. As a coach you need to know the meaning you attach to confrontation, whether you or someone else initiates it. If you don't, you run the risk of becoming victim to your own lack of mindfulness.

Those coaches (or players) who choose to avoid confrontation (the flight response), do not eliminate the problem. In fact, to ignore it tends to intensify it. As it intensifies, the individual finds alternative (and less healthy) ways of dealing with it.

- He broods, which carries over into other situations and relationships.
- He complains to people unrelated to the concern, usually presenting a one-sided point of view, and risks worsening the situation or creating a new one.
- He blows up and says or does something regrettable to the individual with whom he is upset.

Not all coaches (or players) who choose to confront directly do so in a healthy way. Some choose to fight. Generally, they create situations that are reactionary in nature, where one party's behavior triggers a reaction in another. A hard foul, in practice, for example, which is perceived to be deliberate, may lead to a retaliatory push or more. The missing piece of information in this confrontation is the "intent" of the person committing the foul. If that foul simply stood on its own, the intent may have been nothing more than vigorous play, and the teammate on the receiving end may have wrongfully interpreted it otherwise. If, however, the foul was one of a number of hard hits delivered by the player, there may be more behind it than mere vigorous play. In any case, a confrontation has occurred and needs to be resolved.

Not all confrontations are reactionary. Some are planned or intentional confrontations where an event or behavior needs to be addressed in private, where others are not present to alter the dynamics of the confrontation. For example, a coach needs to confront a player for lazy play, which allows opposing players to get down the court or field, putting them in better scoring positions. While the coach may have addressed this issue in practice, perhaps a number of times, this confrontation is one-on-one, more deliberate. The manner in which it is conducted will determine its success.

Before confronting another, you need to consider a couple of points. First, you need to consider in what way people prefer to be confronted. How do they "hear" another person's perception of their flaws or weaknesses? The answer to that question, and the next consideration, is based on the credibility of and the trust they have in the person doing the confronting. Is your perception valuable to them? Do they want to hear what you have to offer?

With those thoughts in mind, you might consider beginning confrontations you need to have by ensuring, to the best of your ability, that you have a good working relationship with the individual being confronted. A particular assistant coach, for example, may have developed a good relationship with a certain player, making him better equipped to talk with that player.

In addition, the most successful confrontations are those that begin with asking the player whether he would like some feedback about his play. That may raise the hackles of some coaches, but consider the benefit of asking that question. When you order players to behave or play a particular way, you send an ultimatum of sorts: "play or don't play." The challenge is often perceived as a threat. Few of us respond well to threats. When you ask a player whether he would like some feedback, you provide a choice. You still hold the control over whether or not to play the athlete, but now, the player has some control, as well. He can listen and learn, or he can continue to play as he has and take the risk of playing less or not at all. When the athlete says that he would like that feedback, he is more apt to listen to what you have to say, especially if the message is delivered in a calm and forthright manner.

Good guidelines to follow when confronting another include:

- Avoid personal attacks, sarcasm, and threats. Your purpose in confronting should be to let that person know what you see, not to hurt him.
- Take responsibility and ownership for your own observations and beliefs about the behavior of concern, understanding that the person may accept or reject your feedback. A person's capacity to objectively evaluate the validity of your observations, to a larger degree, depends on his sense of self-worth.
- Some expressions that facilitate rather than impede healthy confrontation include: "Help me understand," "It seems to me," "I see . . ."

A calm and forthright confronting strategy includes the following four points:

1. *I feel*: Begin by naming the *feeling* you have with regard to the situation. Make certain it is a feeling you have, not a judgment you are making.
2. *I see*: Name the behavior or behaviors about which you take issue. Be specific. It is best not to name more than a couple, since pointing out numerous issues will feel overwhelming to the individual.

3. *I want*: Name your expectation, the behavior you want to see from the person. Again, do not ask for the moon; one or two different behaviors will be challenge enough.

4. *I will*: State what you are willing to do to help facilitate change. You could negotiate what the person would like from you to support that change.

The use of this strategy has been successful for people in their personal, family, and professional lives. It is not a discussion or an argument; it is one person confronting (some call it "care-fronting") another. It may take only a few minutes to complete.

The key for using this kind of strategy is to have it mapped out in your mind before you begin. Know what you will say. Do not allow interruptions. Here is a sample care-fronting:

- *I feel* frustrated with aspects of your behavior on this team.
- *I see* you avoiding eye contact and hear you mumbling negative comments about your teammates when they try to help you. I don't see you encouraging anyone on the team.
- *I want* to see you accept other's encouragement and acknowledge good play by your teammates.
- *I will* help you with that by holding you accountable for becoming a better teammate.

Notice that the coach did not resort to personal attack, sarcasm, or threat. He did provide the athlete with the information and the offer of support he needs to change his behavior. The method by which the coach will hold the athlete accountable may be determined by the two of them. The athlete might make a mental note to add a column to his stat sheet entitled "mental assists," those he gives, those he gets. He may meet with the coach down the road to evaluate the change he is attempting to make. Subsequent confrontations around the same issue will necessitate more stringent "I will" statements. If, after repeated attempts to confront an athlete with poor behavior or performance, no change is made, the coach will do what is best for the program: Put up with, bench, or suspend the player—or kick him off the team.

Healthy confrontation is effective confrontation. It provides the best opportunity for necessary and productive change, and change is essential to the development of young people and athletes.

17

CRITICISM

Criticism, like confrontation, elicits a negative response for many. Unfortunately, if you are going to coach, at any level, it comes with the territory. It comes from all directions: fans, the Internet, letters to the editor, media, parents, and, sometimes, even from team members. Few, if any, other professions are subject to as much criticism as coaching. Because the profession is so public, it is open to more criticism. Also, more people believe themselves to be experts in the field because they either have participated in or watched sports. In their minds, that familiarity validates their criticism.

Some coaches seem less affected by criticism than others. Why is that? Could it be that how a coach receives criticism depends to a large degree on how secure he is with himself? The stronger the belief, the less vulnerable he is. Also, not all criticism is negative. Constructive criticism is valuable, and any coach, if he intends to gain experience and insight in his field, should welcome sound criticism.

Criticism that is not constructive, however, can negatively impact you as a coach. If you are going to work in a profession where criticism is so prevalent, you need to know how to deal with it. I believe you have three choices, generally, in how you choose to respond to negative criticism.

1. Ignore it
2. React to it, usually by attacking in a defensive way.
3. Respond to it in a healthy manner.

I am fairly certain that all coaches have used each of these options at one time or another. I remember ignoring criticism about a player of mine and his off-court behavior because I thought the messenger had an ax to grind, and I did not want to believe the accusations. It turns out the criticism and accusations were valid and the situation became a much bigger problem than it would have if I had taken a look at the criticism and dealt with it.

On another occasion, following a big win, I remember a parent coming to me and saying he wanted to talk to me. Without knowing what he was going to say and expecting it to be negative, I said I had a job to do, and he needed to worry about his job and leave me alone. His response was brief. "I just wanted to tell you I appreciate how you are coaching my son and the team." I was defensive and attacked what I thought was going to be criticism. Needless to say, the parent was not impressed, and our relationship was strained thereafter.

There are implications regardless of the option we choose to take in responding to criticism. Let's look at some of them.

1. Ignore it. What if there is some truth to the criticism? How do you know if the criticism is warranted if you do not examine it? By ignoring the criticism you deny yourself an opportunity to grow and develop.
2. React to it. Usually, when we get defensive, we go on the attack: "Where did he ever coach?" or "I hear he has personal problems." The interaction and relationship become energy draining and unproductive. We have accomplished little, except for venting our anger and frustration. In fact, sometimes we have made the situation worse and may now have an enemy.
3. Respond in a healthy manner. There are several considerations you may take when you choose to respond in this way:
    - Take an objective look at the criticism. Is it something you consistently hear? If the criticism is frequent, it is

probably worth examining. Persistent criticism is a sign of a potential problem. If you examine and decide to operate another way, you've given it good deliberation.

- From whom does the criticism come? Is the criticism from someone you respect for their knowledge of coaching, a member of the coaching staff, a player, or is it from a frustrated fan or parent? Regardless of where it comes from, it is worth examining. Once you look at the criticism, you may find that it is outrageous or silly and can be easily dismissed.

- What are my triggers? As a coach, what is it about which I am sensitive or insecure? Do I overreact? Do I feel disrespected? Whatever our responses, it is not helpful to allow them to thwart potentially useful criticism.

- Is there a ring of truth to the criticism? Often, criticism hurts because there is some truth to it. By recognizing the truth in criticism, you can make a conscious choice to address the issue or not.

It takes a strong and secure person to look at criticism in an objective way. It isn't easy to admit that you are not doing something well, but the willingness to try is the most important step you take. Sometimes, help is necessary. A highly respected colleague, mentor, minister, or sports psychologist may provide the support you need to work through the issue.

The advantage of facing criticism in a healthy way far outweighs the risk. You have an opportunity for growth and for creating a healthier atmosphere for everyone in the program. It may not be easy, but the rewards are invaluable.

18

GAME OFFICIALS

Referees, umpires, and officials are part of the game. Yes, they have a lot of influence in the outcome of the game, but until we come up with a better system, which is unlikely, they are here to stay. A good deal of energy, talk, complaint, and downright nastiness is directed at officials, an unfortunate fact that serves only to distract players and coaches from playing the game. To be successful in competition, a coach must develop a healthy and appropriate way of working with game officials.

The attitude that I, as a coach, have adopted toward officials is based upon several insights and ideas.

1. Most officials are pretty good at what they do. Instant replay has proven that officials, for the most part, make accurate calls, often under challenging circumstances. In fact, even after repeatedly reviewing plays in slow motion, we find that making the right call often proves to be difficult. If we operate from the premise that most officials are competent and professional, we will be less likely to respond heatedly to calls we find questionable.

2. Most officials are officiating honestly. Despite a couple of recent incidents where officials have been professionally dishonest, the majority of them aspire to make accurate calls without partiality.

3. When you ask coaches what they expect from officials, their two most common responses are consistency and impartiality. Unfortunately, though, what some coaches really want is for every call to go their way. Complaints about unfair refereeing intensify after games where one team accrues more penalties than the other, as though officials are obligated to spread the calls evenly despite the manner of play. The fact is some teams are better at drawing fouls and penalties than others.

4. Some coaches overreact to early calls. I once saw a basketball coach get a technical foul before the game started because of a dispute with an official about how much time was placed on the clock for warm-up. I also have observed coaches react violently to calls in the first minute or two of a game. From my perspective, that kind of behavior suggests the coach carries with himself an attitude, a tension, toward officials, which gets triggered early in the contest. A coach puts himself into a better position with officials and with the progression of play if he mentally prepares himself for potentially disputable calls.

5. Talk to officials appropriately. Coaches have a right to advocate for their teams with game officials, but the manner in which they do it determines the effectiveness of that advocacy. A coach who constantly complains or screams at officials loses his credibility with those officials. A coach who talks reasonably with officials about calls that seem obviously wrong or who asks for rule interpretations is more likely to be heard.

6. Each referee and umpire has his own style of officiating. Coaches must adjust to those individual differences. Some umpires, for example, have a broader strike zone range, which may influence a coach's decision about giving the swing-away sign on the 2-0 count. Some basketball referees allow more contact, which may influence what the defense a coach will use or the players he will play. Don't waste energy trying to change an official. Instead, adjust.

7. Coach your team. Very simply, you have too much to do coaching your team during a game to expend time and energy dealing with officials. Think of the number of times you have seen a basketball coach, with five seconds to go in a tight game, spend the entire time-out arguing with the referee over a previous call. At this point, the game is about the next play, not the last one.

8. Officials will not make every call correct. You will get bad calls and sometimes over the course of the game they will not even out. However, over a longer period of time the good and bad calls are almost exactly even. So to spend a lot of time on the bad calls is fruitless and unproductive.

9. Holding grudges against certain officials is also unproductive. In high school, you often see the same official game after game, the same is true at the college and professional level. To let a bad call by an official a week ago, a month ago, or last year affect your attitude toward that official and the game is not doing you or your team any good.

10. Evaluate officials. Not all officials are good. There are a few who don't seem to have a feel of the game; they do not work well with coaches and players; they use poor judgment in making calls. Evaluate them. Rate them. Speak about them to the director of league officials. Follow the procedure and evaluate officials honestly.

To get a better perspective of the impact game officials have on the game, go to a game in which you have no interest, a game you can watch objectively. I think you will be surprised to see how little effect an official has on the game.

When I look back, I regret the amount of power I gave officials. I realize now that I would have been better served focusing on coaching my team. To do otherwise sets a poor example for your team.

Coaching is far more enjoyable when you do not waste your time and energy complaining about or fretting over officials. Concentrate on what you can control and work on developing appropriate ways of working with officials. That effort most effectively supports your team.

4TH QUARTER:

EXAMINE COACHING STYLES, TECHNIQUES, AND IDEAS

19

PASSION/ENERGY COACH OR TECHNIQUE/DETAIL COACH

As a coach, the way you conduct your practices is crucial for the success of the team. You want your players to understand and have confidence in what you are doing and be able to transfer that to the game situation. There are many different ways to teach and to conduct a practice.

The style of ball your team plays will factor into the type and length of practice you have. Some coaches are firm believers in drill work, others in scrimmaging. Some coaches believe in highly intense, energetic practices, while others are into teaching all of the little details and techniques involved in building a skill. Still others believe in trying to do both. It is important to examine what you believe in as a coach to get your team best prepared. There is a line, and it is important for you to know where you stand on that line.

To better understand some of the differences I've mentioned, let's take a look at two very successful coaches in college basketball: Tom Izzo, of Michigan State, and Rick Majerus, of St. Louis, (previously of Ball State and Utah). I have attended several practices of Coach Izzo. His practices are very intense, and tough. He believes in developing and pushing players to be physical and hard-nosed. On the other hand, Coach Majerus stresses technique and detail. That is not to say Coach Izzo does not teach and pay attention to detail. He does; in fact, the scouting his staff does and provides to the players is significant. Also, anyone who has seen Coach Majerus's teams play realizes they play physical and tough. So what is the difference?

To clarify, let's use, as an example, a basketball player on defense trying to control the dribbler—not allowing him to penetrate. I believe Izzo's approach would promote hard work, toughness, and determination, with some teaching of stance and footwork, to get the job done. Majerus's approach would emphasis stance, footwork, and scouting the opponent, and having the toughness and determination to go with it. Both are teaching the same things but with more emphasis in one area than another and starting from different places.

Each style of teaching carries its own benefits and detriments.

Passion/Energy Approach

Benefits

- Players develop an attitude of never backing down.
- Players feed off one another's energy.
- Hustle and toughness are skills they practice daily.

Detriments

- Teams can get tired, especially late in the season.
- If the game becomes more of a chess match it slows down, and energy and passion are less important.
- Sometimes when patience and mental discipline are needed, they are not emphasized.
- The emotional tides can be rocky. When things go bad, sometimes the spirit and passion go away.

Detail/Technique Approach

Benefits

- The team is prepared for almost anything that can happen in a game.
- The team is fundamentally sound, forcing the other team to beat you; you will not beat yourself.
- The players feel they are better coached than their opponents.

Detriments

- Players think too much about technique and forget to just play.
- Sometimes the passion and energy are not there.

The approach you use as a coach depends a lot on what sport you are coaching. Coaching a golfer or a bowler requires more teaching of technique and detail than team sports. Even in team sports, though, certain aspects require more emphasis on teaching than passion and toughness. In basketball, generally, offense requires more teaching of detail and technique than defense. However, both are needed at each end of the court.

You, as a coach, will gravitate toward a particular style of play, but like Coaches Izzo and Majerus, you will need to create a balance in order to ensure success.

20

COACH BY FEAR/INTIMIDATION OR ACCOUNTABILITY/ DISCIPLINE

Whenever I do consulting work and evaluate a program, I ask myself three questions: Is this a place in which I would want to work? Is this a program in which I would want my son or daughter to participate? Does this program challenge the players and give them the support they need to achieve at a high level in the athletic arena, the academic arena, and in life? Fortunately, in most programs that I have worked, I can answer yes to all three. To do this, the program and coach would have to operate and function using accountability and discipline as the staple of the program rather than fear and intimidation. Let's take a look at both.

I read a newspaper quote by a very successful coach (successful, at least, by his W-L record) who said he coaches by fear and intimidation. I do not know whether or not the quote was accurate, but I believe many coaches do coach that way. When you coach by fear and intimidation, you are basically holding leverage over the athlete, threatening him. When you walk onto the court or field, you want the athletes to know you are there, you control them, and you have the power. You may use their job security, scholarship, playing time as reasons why they better do as you demand.

Playing mind games with athletes is also a form of coaching by fear and intimidation. Putting them through tests every day to see how much adversity and grief they can handle is an example of a coach controlling the players. Of course players need to be challenged and learn to deal with adversity, not simply because the coach wants the athlete to know that he is in charge but to prepare them for difficult times in games. An example would be in practice during a scrimmage to make bad refereeing calls against the starting team, simulating what happens in games sometimes.

A number of coaches have been successful (i.e., have a good W-L record) coaching by fear and intimidation. However, I believe some significant difficulties surface using this method.

1. It is not much fun. The experience is not that enjoyable for the athlete, and, sometimes, not for the assistant coaches and support staff.
2. It is hard to keep your coaching job coaching that way over the long term. Coaching by fear and intimidation wears on people; they get sick of it and no longer support it.
3. Members of the program (players, assistant coaches, support staff) are walking on egg shells. They are afraid what they are doing may be criticized. When people are functioning that way, it is often times hard for them to operate at their full capacity.
4. You had better win. People will tolerate more if the team is winning; when you start losing under this method, people tend to turn on the coach. The aggravation does not seem worth it to them.

Holding an athlete accountable and establishing discipline are necessary in building a top-notch program. Coaching with accountability and discipline is much different from coaching with fear and intimidation. Accountability means following the rules: Be on time, touch the lines in wind sprints, have the shirt tucked in, and focus on the coach when he is talking. Accountability also means running out fly balls full speed, running pass patterns full speed when the play is not for you. If an athlete is not accountable, disciplinary action may be called for: running extra wind sprints, being replaced, losing a starting position. The key is that there are expectations that, when not met, result in consequences. The coach does not threaten, try to scare, and intimidate the athlete. He simply holds him accountable.

Accountability means following the rules, and discipline means enforcing those rules. I believe a coach can teach much more when using accountability and discipline than when using intimidation. It is important for coaches to be consistent in holding players accountable and applying discipline. The players need to know accountability does not change from day to day, nor from player to player. As coaches we can communicate expectations to our players and support them in reaching those expectations. Those expectations are not about simply being successful in the win column. They are about being successful as part of the team and in life. Ultimately, as a coach we want to teach and assist athletes to become self-accountable and self-disciplined. When that happens, the opportunity for success, in all areas, greatly increases.

When you use accountability and discipline as a coaching method, you can use a more positive tone. I believe the athlete will feel that the coach is with him in that case. When you use fear and intimidation, it is almost always done in a negative way. It often becomes coach against player, player against coach. In general, I believe athletes respond to positive methods better than negative methods.

Often, you will hear coaches say, "I don't care if my players like me as long as they respect me." Although I think respect for the coach is of great importance, I believe having players like the coach is important as well. When a player likes *and* respects a coach, he is more likely to try and do what that coach wants and more likely to give all of himself for the team and the coach. I suspect when a player does not like a coach, he may demonstrate respect, but he does not truly respect the coach.

The benefits of holding athletes accountable and instilling discipline outweigh the time necessary to achieve that.

1. Everybody understands the rules and requirements. When they mess up, they understand. They may not like it, but they know what is coming.

2. Athletes want discipline. They may not act like it, but they realize for the team and themselves to be successful, they need it.
3. The atmosphere is much healthier than under a dictator.
4. Winning, of course, is important, but the experience can still be positive when times are tough.
5. Players are more likely to stick with the coach.
6. You can coach long term this way.

How do you coach? Do you coach by fear and intimidation or by accountability and discipline? Making the commitment to coach using accountability and discipline is more enjoyable and more productive—for everyone in the program.

21

PLAY ME—I'LL SHOW YOU, OR SHOW ME—I'LL PLAY YOU

Generally, players and coaches think differently when it comes to determining playing time. Players have the attitude, play me—I'll show you. Coaches are of the mind, show me—I'll play you. I believe it is important for both player and coach to understand how the other thinks.

In addition to a difference of mind-set between players and coaches, we see a difference in performance among players in practice and games. Coaches agree that it would be ideal if players performed consistently in practice and in games. Unfortunately, many do not. One player may look great in practice but freeze in games. I had a college teammate we called "Three o'clock." He was awesome at three o'clock in practice, but most of our games were in the evening. Another kind of player, sometimes referred to as a "gamer," performs adequately in practice but at game time when the lights come on, so does the player.

If we take a closer look at the player who looks great in practice but struggles in games, we find, typically, a player who comes prepared to practice every day, who does the drills, and runs the plays correctly. Usually, this player understands the game, what the coach wants, and probably has learned and adjusted to his teammates' moves in practice. However, come game time he may get nervous, lack confidence, and have trouble adjusting to the moves of his opponents. The lack of familiarity troubles him.

The "play me—I'll show you" player, typically, is not a very good practice player. He has trouble paying attention to detail, is likely to get bored, and may not be very disciplined. He approaches practice like it is something he has to do to play the game. However, come game time, he plays confidently and aggressively and, in general, steps up his game.

What you see in practice may not be what you get in games. Coaches understand this. Darrin Horn, the basketball coach at the University of South Carolina, tells his team, "As your coach, I want to know what I am getting, meaning that when I put you into the game, I want to know what to expect." Of course, all coaches strive toward that objective, but with some players that prediction is harder to make than with others.

Working with inconsistent players requires some examination of the situation. Consider how much opportunity you are going to give the guy who does not practice as well you would like but plays well in games. Are you going to bend at all? Is it acceptable to you if you play him when, in fact, he does not seem to earn playing time in practice? Or perhaps that playing time depends on why he does not practice as well as you would like. Is the reason based on attitude, desire, attention, focus, concentration, or understanding the game? If he makes improvement but still falls below your standards in practice, will he get playing time? These questions need to be explored. The answers for one coach may be different from another.

Find ways to demonstrate how much better the "play me—I'll show you" guy could be if he becomes a "show me—I'll play you" guy. Help him to see how poor practice affects his performance in the game. For example, show him in what ways not knowing the scouting report and not understanding team concepts affects his playing time. Examine his reasons, those about which he is aware and those about which you may make an educated guess, for poor practice play. Develop a plan to address those.

Show confidence and belief in the player who practices well and is prepared. Find ways to take his practice play into the game.

Perhaps certain game situations are better suited for him, situations where his knowledge of the game and preparation is helpful. This type of player probably plays better when he is comfortable knowing what the other team is doing. For example, attacking zone defenses or defending set offenses in basketball or blocking a standard nonblitzing defense in football. This player will make mistakes and need you to stick with him in tough times.

Determine what is best for the team. As a coach, you need to provide balance for the team, being neither too stubborn nor too lax in establishing and reinforcing expectations for your players. The clearer and the more respectful the communication, the more likely those expectations will be met.

22

PLAY TO WIN OR
NOT TO LOSE

There is a difference between playing to win and playing not to lose. In general, playing to win means being aggressive, offensively minded, and taking more chances. Playing not to lose means taking fewer chances, being defensively minded, and waiting for the other team to make a mistake. Neither method (or idea) is right or wrong. But it is important for a coach to take stock and determine which way he leans and which way gives his team the best chance for success.

Consider the following situations in competition and decide which method you as a coach or athlete might choose.

- *Golf*: Hit approach shots at the pin or at the safe side of the green. Try to make 20-foot putts and risk going by the hole 4 or 5 feet or lag putts up.
- *Football*: Have a 14-point lead in the fourth quarter and continue to pass up field or run the ball to keep the clock moving.
- *Basketball*: Have a 10- to 12-point lead with four minutes to go in the game, continue to fast break, and do not use the shot clock. Or use the shot clock.
- *Tennis*: Try to hit winning shots, or get the ball back over the net, waiting for the opponent to make a mistake.

Knowing when and how much to play to win is crucial for a coach to be successful. It seems to me there is a line, and as a coach you need to determine where you stand on that line. Most coaches, I suspect, are fairly close to the line—just on one side or the other. Some coaches, however, are quite far from the line on one side or the other. Of course, the line may change from game to game or even *during* the game.

There are pros and cons to each style of play.

Play to win

Pros

- The game can be a lot of fun.
- The athlete and team can develop confidence.
- The athlete and team can experience positive momentum.
- The athlete and team believe that the result of the game is in their hands; they have control.
- The athlete and team can play more freely, less restricted.

Cons

- There may be a lot of ups and downs in the game.
- It is easier to lose big.
- Your team play may not be very effective if the other team is more talented.

Play not to lose

Pros

- Your team usually can stay closer longer in the game against a talented team.
- Your team is less likely to get way behind.
- It forces your opponent to make plays.

Cons

- It is more difficult to get as many big plays.
- Outcome of the game is more in the opponents' hands.
- Players may sense the coach lacks confidence in them.

There are many examples of athletes and teams who have won and lost big games playing both ways. A good example of playing to win and being too aggressive was Jean van de Velde in the 1999 British Open. Going into the 18th hole of the final day, Van de Velde needed only to get a double bogey or less to win. He kept the pedal to medal, choosing to hit the driver off the tee. Even then, after a poor drive, he still had plenty of opportunity to play conservatively and not lose. He chose otherwise and made triple bogey, and eventually lost in the playoff.

Conversely, we often see teams get ahead and try to hang on and let the clock run out. One high school team I coached had a 12-point lead with three minutes to go in the game. I instructed them to shoot only layups. We started to play uptight in an effort not to lose, which we eventually did in overtime.

As a coach you need to take an honest assessment of your position on this issue with each team you coach.

- Do I instill confidence in my team? Do I allow my players to rely on and trust their instincts to continue to make plays in the crucial time of the game? Or do I express a lack of confidence in my team? Do I try to hang on to the lead, control and constrain my players during crucial times in the game?
- Where do I stand on the line? Ask coaching friends and assistants to see how they view you.
- After determining where you are on the line, ask yourself about your tendencies in tight games situations. Make a concerted effort to adjust those tendencies if that is warranted.
- Experiment in practicing in different ways. For example, shoot more/fewer 3s in basketball. Pass more/less in football. Shoot more/fewer shots at the pin in golf.

I think that if you polled coaches, most would say they play to win. They will say their team plays aggressively and attacks; that's how they would like to think of themselves and their team.

In reality, I think that may not be true. Many coaches, I believe, play not to lose. Comments like, "We just want to be in the game with three minutes to go" or "If I had more talent we would press and fast break more" are examples of coaches playing not to lose. The important thing is not to see yourself one way but do it another way.

Questions to ask yourself as a coach:

1. Do I play to win?
2. If I play to win, do I sometimes overdo it?
3. Do I play not to lose?
4. If I play not to lose, do I sometimes overdo it?

23

POSITIVE PRETALK OR NEGATIVE POST-TALK

During the fall of the 2007–2008 basketball season, I had a conversation with Darrin Horn, then head basketball coach at Western Kentucky (now of the University of South Carolina). He told me about a conditioning drill he had his team do. Normally, they did five sets of the drill, but, on one occasion, he told them that the next day they were going to do seven sets. Immediately, he sensed that they were convinced it was going to be too hard and practically impossible for most to succeed. So, for the next ten to fifteen minutes, Coach Horn talked with his players about why they would succeed and how they were going to do it. He talked about how an athlete can push himself beyond where he thinks he can go, how that night they were going to visualize themselves succeeding, and how they were going to support, encourage, and hold teammates accountable.

The next day, all but two of the players completed the seven sets, and those two achieved more than they ever had before. When I asked Darrin whether he thought his players would have done as well if he had not had that talk with them, his answer was no. When I asked him if he had not talked to them, and they had done poorly on the drill, how he would have handled it. He said, "I probably would have had a meeting with them, and told them the workout was disappointing, and they were capable of more." As we discussed this, we agreed that positive pretalk is usually much more powerful than negative post-talk.

How many times in athletics have you or someone you know delivered a long, heated tongue-lashing following a disappointing game while media, friends, and family waited outside the locker room? Have you ever taken that long bus trip back home after a loss only to go into the locker room for a lengthy meeting while the coach laments about the team? Most times, very little is accomplished in those situations apart from providing the coach an opportunity to vent his frustration (see chapter 7, "What Is Your Motivation?"). Often more damage than benefit comes from those talks. That is why a lot of coaches have the 24 rule: For 24 hours, they do not say anything that they may regret later.

The 24 rule aside, some coaches, thinking they will provoke their team into playing better, carry their negative message into the pretalk of the next game. Too often, that negativity becomes a pattern and the players learn not to listen.

Positive pretalk is so much more effective than negative post-talk. When I speak of positive pretalk, I am not necessary referring to a motivational speech, although that may be part of it. Motivational speeches take you only so far and so often. I'm referring to the talk that puts the athlete in the proper frame of mind so he achieves as close to his potential as possible, the kind of speech Coach Horn had with his team to prepare them for the conditioning drill.

The best example of positive pretalk I was involved with occurred during the day-before-the-game meeting Coach Tom Crean, of Marquette (now the coach of Indiana University), had with his team before playing Kentucky to advance to the Final Four in 2003. The talk by Coach Crean was done in a calm, steady voice, but it proved to be motivational because he inspired his team to believe. He explained to his team that they were going to play well the next day because they were prepared. He explained to them they were going to play well not because they *should* count on each other, but because they knew they *could* count on each other. He explained to them that they were going to play well because they trusted each other and because they did not care who got the attention and glory. Then he emphasized to them that because they were going to play well, the results would take care of themselves: They would win because they were the better team. There was not a person in that room that did not believe in what he said. The talk was positive. Although Kentucky was the favorite, Marquette won convincingly. There was no need for negative post-talk.

Of course, the results are not always what we want, even after positive pretalk. However, the odds for success improve if we can convince our team and players that they are capable of achieving. Sometimes, the players and the coach do not truly believe. When that happens, we need to work at the positive pretalk, or as some say fake it until you make it. You do it enough, it can become real.

The words any coach uses are effective only insomuch as they inspire or reinforce belief. Negative words reinforce that no matter what I do, I cannot achieve or please or succeed. They invoke fear. Positive words reinforce the belief that I am capable. I can succeed. They invoke confidence.

Questions to ask yourself as a coach:

1. How much of my coaching communication is negative?
2. How much of my coaching communication is positive?
3. Do I do too much of postgame negative talk?
4. Do I do enough of pregame positive talk?

24

STICK TO YOUR GUNS

"Stick to your guns." "Be determined to make it work." "Believe in what you do and how you do it without hesitation or deviation." "Do not get sidetracked." Convictions like these may be commendable. When they evolve from strong principles and experience, they provide a foundation from which to work. When they evolve from fear or an unreasonable need for control, however, they become law unto themselves.

Living in the Raleigh-Durham area I had an opportunity to follow closely the charges of rape against three Duke University lacrosse players in 2006. Initially, many in the community were outraged at the three players regarding the alleged crime. Slowly, though, the facts, or lack of facts, indicated that rape had not occurred. Eventually, as most people know, all charges were dropped and the district attorney was disbarred. Later, we were told the district attorney, entrenched in his belief that the young men were guilty, refused to listen to anyone who had reservations about that guilt. The issue for him, it seems, centered on the control he had on the case rather than on the veracity of the testimony. He became unreasonably and obstructively determined to prevail.

Coaches, too, can become unreasonably and obstructively determined to prevail and refuse even to listen to the contributions of their own coaching staffs. Sticking to their guns (or operating from an unstable belief system) turns into holding others prisoners to your own way of thinking and operating. It means staying with the offense or defense, refusing to make adjustments, even if warranted. The program becomes rigid and, contrary to the intentions of the coach, more inclined to crack.

An effective program is a flexible program. That does not mean one throws out the convictions upon which it is built. It does mean one is open to and evaluates the benefits of change within those convictions.

Recognizing your own customary behaviors will help ensure that changes you make are sound and less likely to be the result of your own biases. As you consider making changes in your program or coaching style, ask yourself the following questions:

- How objective am I? Do I know my biases? Am I impulsive or unusually slow to change?
- Do I have the ability to look at facts, statistics, logic or use common sense when making decisions? Am I inclined to ignore those things?
- Am I willing to take an objective look at aspects of myself or my program and let the findings take me wherever they may go?
- Can members of my staff or my players offer an opinion or idea without fear of being criticized or called disloyal?

Had the district attorney asked himself these questions, the whole Duke lacrosse case might have played out differently, with fewer people hurt and fewer lives shattered.

Great coaches have strong ideas and plans for their programs and how they run them. But they also are not afraid to consider changes or adjustments that may need to be made from time to time.

25

CHOOSE TO SEE STRENGTHS
INSTEAD OF WEAKNESSES

It is common for those of us in athletics to focus on what we or our athletes lack. I would like to have a dime for every time a coach complained to me about what was lacking in his program or in his players.

We coaches are with our players a good deal of time: training and conditioning programs, practice, and games. We get to know them well—their strengths and weaknesses. Often, we tend to see their warts, their flaws, and their shortcomings all too easily. And these are all the more conspicuous when things are not going well during a practice or a game.

We tend to see events and people as we see ourselves, positively, negatively, or somewhere in between. If we are inclined to focus on our own limitations, we will look for those in others, as well. While we cannot change easily or quickly those internal messages under which we operate, we do have a choice in how and what we communicate. We have to work at focusing on the strengths.

1. Accept your players. Whether you or someone else recruited them for your college team or they walked onto the floor in the high school gym, they are your players. Do not wish for others. Those players on the other teams that look so good have their own issues and limitations.

2. Recognize the skills in each player. They do have skills; it is your responsibility to identify and cultivate them. Let the athlete know that you see and appreciate the value of those skills and the athlete himself.

3. Help the player develop his skill. Accentuate the positive. Generally, as a player works to improve an existing skill, there will be some degree of carryover to other related skills. Minimize the effects of weaknesses. Ignoring an athlete's weaknesses is counterproductive. However, you can approach that weakness in a productive manner. Rather than putting a glaring spotlight on it for the purpose of judging, use it as a point of information: "That pass did not work well in that situation; how about using..."

4. Choose to emphasize how to use an athlete in competition rather than only to improve his weak skills. Place athletes in situations where they are most likely to have success. Asking a strong, slow running back to run end sweeps and reverses does not make much sense. When we ask athletes to perform in ways contrary to their abilities, we lead them to frustration.

And often times, by seeing and pointing out the weaknesses of the players or team, the coach is building an excuse for himself to not take responsibility. A good example of a coach who chose not to do that, who chose to see the strengths not the weaknesses, was Rick Pitino, of the University of Kentucky, in 1992 and 1993. He did not recruit many, if any of the players on the team, but he adopted them as his own, and adapted to them. That particular Kentucky team was not real big and strong, but they were an outstanding pressing and shooting team. Coach Pitino installed a press and had his team shoot many three-pointers, which allowed them to play to their strengths. His 1992 and 1993 teams were very successful, getting to the Elite Eight and the Semifinals, respectively, in the NCAA tournament.

Regardless of our best efforts, there will be some cases when no matter how many positives a coach gives an athlete, that athlete anticipates and hears best the negative. It is as though he knows that what is valued most by the coach is that which he lacks as an athlete. Athletes, and assistant coaches for that matter, who look for criticism in this way, as a form of disapproval, live under some pretty heavy internal censure. Changing the underlying beliefs that precipitate that kind of censure cannot be done on the playing field or in the locker room. We can, however, choose to communicate in ways that do not fuel them. While the athlete or coach may not be able to hear the positive in our message, we will know that, to the best of our ability, we have been supportive and respectful in our communication.

26

IMPROVE COMPETITIVENESS

Most athletes like to think of themselves as highly competitive, and compared to the average person, they probably are. In reality, it is the exception rather than the rule to have highly competitive players—those who love to win and hate to lose when they step onto the field or floor.

There are, of course, exceptions. I have been fortunate to have been associated with some athletes whose competitiveness stood out in a highly competitive atmosphere. The one that readily comes to mind is Travis Diener, a point guard with the Indiana Pacers, whom I worked with when he played at Marquette University. Some people are more competitive because of their nature, experience, or upbringing. Travis comes from a family of athletes and coaches, where competition was ever-present. He and his cousins Drew, who played at St. Louis University, and Drake, who played at DePaul University, were constantly competing against each other. Travis, was the type of athlete who did a solid job during fundamental drills in practice, but when the lights went on or score was being kept he became totally immersed in winning.

Dwyane Wade, of the Miami Heat, is also known for his competitive nature, but I believe he learned much of it during his days at Marquette from his coach, Tom Crean, and from Travis Diener. Tom Izzo, basketball coach at Michigan State University, credits Mateen Cleaves, the point guard of the 2002 NCAA national championship team, with imposing his will on the other members of his team. Having guys on your team like Wade, Diener, and Cleaves is exciting because their competitiveness carries over to other members of the team.

These guys are exceptions to the rule, to be sure, but why is that? Before we can understand how to create and develop a more competitive team, I think it is necessary to see why more people are not as competitive as we coaches would like. I suspect a number of factors contribute to that.

1. Our society emphasizes self-esteem, self-worth, having young people feel good about themselves. Today, young people are rewarded for participating not for achieving. Whether you like it or not, that is the reality.
2. Playgrounds and outdoor activities have become obsolete; today, kids play on the computer. If they lose a game, they just hit the reset button and start again. There is no pain or suffering with the loss.
3. Organized sports such as AAU basketball and summer baseball programs provide a seemingly unending opportunity for another game. You as an individual or a team are guaranteed to play in the losers' bracket, or the toilet bowl, and there's always next weekend.
4. A lot of great competitors feel isolated, sometimes disliked and criticized for being competitive. Their competitiveness is perceived as negative. It takes a strong person to overcome the pressure and stigma placed on them.

That is not to say promoting self-esteem, developing self-worth, AAU basketball, and summer baseball, are bad and do not have any value. Of course, they do. They have many positive impacts, but they can also have negative impacts when it comes to developing competitiveness.

If the end result of these influences has been to reduce the competitive spirit of athletes, how do coaches teach competitiveness?

- Hustle. Hustle is not necessary for competitiveness, but it is a start. By teaching hustle, you have an athlete trying hard, which can lead to competitiveness. Once, when coaching a high school basketball team, I decided as a coach to see how many times we could dive on the floor for a loose ball, to see how good we could get at it. So for three days we practiced *hustle*, mostly by diving on the floor for loose balls. We also kept statistics on how we were doing; we made it competitive. The kids bought in completely. Come game time Friday, we were not only outstanding in our hustle, but we also competed much harder in other aspects of the game, like defense and rebounding. The loose ball mentality carried over to other phases of the game.

- Loving to win. Loving to win means preparing to win. It means practicing hard with a purpose. An example would be Virginia Tech's football team and the emphasis they place on their specialty teams. They prepare very diligently in all four special team areas. They take great pride in being successful in those areas, and they usually are. When you prepare for something, come game time, you take pride in your competitiveness in that area. The more you invest, the more you go for it. The more you care, the more competitive you are.

- Hating to lose. Hating to lose means the thought of losing, the taste, the feel, is so ugly that you don't ever want that feeling again. When you get that feeling, the opportunity for the competitive level to increase for the next game is improved. If you let your team accept losing or make excuses for them, the lose will not sting so much, and it's less likely they will be as competitive the next game as you would like. As coaches, we can help athletes learn to hate to lose by not just moving on as if everything is okay, making things comfortable. Having players watch film, replay plays, although painful, helps reinforce the ugliness of the loss and instills the desire to avoid that the next game.

- Competitive drills. Athletes need to practice competing. Have competitive drills; make as many drills and as much of practice as competitive as possible. Keep score; have winners and losers. Reward winners; losers pay the price—run laps and wind sprints, especially when they do not compete as hard as they can.

- Acknowledging competitors on your team. Praise them; use their competitiveness as standards for others on the team. Darrin Horn, the basketball coach at the University of South Carolina, does an awesome job of teaching competitiveness. I have heard him many times after practice or a game, praise someone who maybe did not shoot well but helped the team with his competitive play. He acknowledges competitors.

Making a commitment to improve competitiveness in your program, instead of complaining about the lack of it, is coaching proactively and positively.

27

EVALUATE NONATHLETIC SKILLS

When coaches evaluate players, they look at athletic skills, such as running, jumping, quickness, and vertical leap. And they look at body type, height, and weight. Checklists are available for a coach's use in collecting and using that information.

Another kind of information, however, may be even more helpful as a predictor of a player's success in the program. His nonathletic skill, his character and personality traits speak to his maturity and promise, both athletically and personally.

A coach may gather that kind of information by using several tools: his own observations, others' observations, and an informational checklist.

- By watching how the athlete responds to and reacts in game and other situations, a coach gets a picture of his perspective, sense of self, interaction with others, motivation, and discipline. In the high school setting, this can be done almost on a daily basis. In college recruiting, this may be observed during home visits, campus visits, and during practice and games.
- By talking with people associated with the athlete, a coach can get a feel for how the athlete is perceived by others, both positively and negatively.

- By developing a checklist to be used as an informational tool, the coach will have data to support or discount the information he collects through observations.

Determining Potential

The following checklist is one means of gathering information concerning a team member or potential team member. It is divided into four areas: relational, stability, coachability, and motivational.

- *Relational* refers to the athlete's ability and desire to work with and get along with others.
- *Stability* refers to how mature and emotionally fit the athlete is.
- *Coachability* refers to whether the athlete wants and accepts coaching.
- *Motivational* refers to whether the athlete has inner drive and wants to improve.

Coaches will value each of the four areas (and each item within an area) differently. As a coach, it is important to determine what value each of the areas holds for you.

Take the checklist and apply it to your present and past teams. The conclusions you draw should be helpful to you in the future selection and recruitment for your team. It also will help you evaluate your existing team. If you have a team full of players that score yes in most areas, you probably have a successful group of athletes who achieve at a high standard and are fun to coach. If you have a team with several players who score no in a number of areas, you have some problems to address on an underachieving team.

Relational

- Is the athlete enjoyable to be around?
- Is the athlete respectful to people?
- Does the athlete like being part of the team?

Stability

- Is the athlete low maintenance?
- Is the athlete unselfish?

- Is the athlete mature?
- Is the athlete unspoiled?
- Does the athlete take academics seriously?
- Does the athlete have healthy training habits?
- Is the athlete an energy giver?
- Is the athlete's family situation healthy?

Coachability

- Does the athlete handle injuries well?
- Is the athlete competitive?
- Is the athlete physically tough?
- Is the athlete mentally tough?
- Is the athlete confident?
- Can the athlete take criticism?

Motivational

- Does the athlete like to practice?
- Does the athlete like to work on his game?
- Does the athlete like to do the extra—films, weights, nutrition, and so on.
- Does the athlete have self-pride?

Each week, in my hometown, Raleigh, North Carolina, a local television station honors a high school athlete as Player of the Week. I was watching when a female basketball player was the honoree. The TV reporter interviewed her coach and some of her teachers. They all had the same thing to say, "What a great attitude she has." When the young lady was informed by the reporter of what her coach and teachers said, her comment was, "If you don't have a good attitude, why would people want to be around you?" That statement says a lot. It is fun to be around people with a good attitude. The checklist above will help you find athletes who have a attitude, which goes a long way toward helping your team achieve success.

28

THINK OUTSIDE THE BOX

Some coaches, more creative than others, are not afraid to experiment or let go of conventional wisdom and methods. They think "outside the box." For example, years ago most every basketball coach preached to players not to throw crosscourt passes, fearing interceptions. Now skip passes (crosscourt passes) are an accepted way to attack defenses, especially zone defenses. Years ago, basketball coaches taught their players never to let their man go baseline, to make him go middle; that way they could get help. What coaches did not seem to consider was that when the man went middle he had so many more options. Bobby Knight, at that time the head coach of Indiana, was the first (or one of the first) to instruct his defense to keep the ball out of the middle, the lane. Now, many coaches accept the philosophy of Knight regarding defense. Knight and his counterparts thought outside the box.

Football also has had coaches who, thinking outside of the box, broke away from traditional wisdom. A common philosophy in football is that you must be able to run the ball first to have an effective passing game. The run sets up the pass. Today, many coaches use the pass to set up the run. In fact, a couple of years ago, in an NFL play-off game, one offensive coordinator had his team pass thirty-four out of thirty-six plays—quite successfully, I might add. Why the change? Change occurred when coaches like Steve Spurrier, then of the University of Florida, and the late Bill Walsh, of the San Francisco 49ers, and others, were willing to try different strategies to enable their offense to be more effective.

How about practicing halftime? How often do we see a team come out flat after halftime, after having the momentum going into halftime. There is a skill to coming out, warming up for about three minutes, and being ready to go. Why not practice it? Practice for about one hour, go into the locker room for about ten to twelve minutes, simulating halftime, warm up for about three minutes, and then practice for another hour. Just like a game. Makes sense, but most coaches don't do it.

There are advantages to thinking outside the box. It may give the extra edge for which you are looking. Other teams may have to adjust if you play somewhat out of the norm. About ten or fifteen years ago, there was not a team in the country in college basketball on NCAA selection night that wanted to draw Princeton. Their coach, Pete Carril, had developed a style of offense of three-point shooting and back door layups that scared opponents to death. Coach Carril, realizing that he would probably not be able to recruit the top players in the country, thought outside the box and developed a system that created distress for his opponents. The same is true of Coach Paul Westhead's Loyola Marymount teams of the late Hank Gathers and Bo Kimble. Their style of run-and-gun was very difficult for teams to prepare for.

Sometimes it really isn't thinking outside the box but, rather, playing a more unconventional way that changes the game. For example, in college basketball one decision a coach must make is whether to foul or not when up three points with five or fewer seconds to go in the game and the other team has the ball. A majority of the coaches prefer not to foul, to guard the three-point shot tough. A few coaches will foul, not allowing the opponent to shoot the three. The conventional method is not to foul; the unconventional method is to foul.

Let's take a closer look at the foul-or-not-to-foul debate. If you do not foul, the offensive team has to do one thing to tie the game: make a three-pointer. If you foul with two to three seconds to go, they have to do three things: make the first free throw, miss the second free throw and get the rebound, and make the shot to tie the game. We can argue both sides of the debate, but I believe most coaches prefer not to foul because it is more conventional, and probably does not require so much practice as fouling requires. When you decide to foul, you are going to have to practice to make sure it is not a shooting foul, and foul with only a couple seconds left in the game. I do not believe there is any statistical date to support fouling or not, but as a coach it would be important to practice and experiment with both,

I believe there are several reasons why coaches do not think outside of the box or try new and unconventional methods:

- They are not trained to do so. Young coaches are eager to learn from more experienced veteran coaches. These coaches, however, are often pretty set in their ways and less likely to try new ideas.
- It takes courage. To play a style not many others use, try a fancy play, or do something out of the ordinary makes a coach vulnerable to criticism. If it does not work, the fans, parents, media, and others are more critical than if a coach had used a more traditional method. I believe that is one reason a lot of coaches do not foul at the end of a game; the criticism is much more intense if it does not work.
- There is a lack of trust in the relationships with staff and players. Trust, in general, must be evident throughout the program to try new strategies successfully. When that trust is present, staff and players will support the coach's decision. If that relationship is not present, the coach will not get the support he needs to make it work.

Coaches can learn to think outside the box and become more creative. Here are six suggestions to achieve creativity and flexibility:

1. Constantly think about the team. What can we do differently?

2. Be an idea guy. Throw out ideas, weird lineups, new plays, and people playing different positions. Understand that 90 percent of your ideas probably will be thrown away and never tried, but if one sticks and works, it was worth the effort.
3. Brainstorm. Sit down with your staff and tell them it is crazy idea time. In chapter 3, assistant coaches are encouraged to think through their ideas. Not in a brainstorm session. Throw anything and everything into the ring.
4. Feel the atmosphere and environment. Trust your instincts. I once stopped a basketball practice after fifteen minutes of practice, put up the volleyball net, and had the team play volleyball. It worked. They needed a break and were more than ready to practice the next day.
5. Try new things in practice. Block an off-tackle play in a totally new way; try scoring on offense in basketball in the first ten seconds you have the ball; try to hit winning shots in tennis on every return.
6. Try new drills. If your team is not accomplishing something, try new drills and teaching methods to get the concepts across.

We never will know whether new ideas work if we do not generate and try them. Keeping yourself creative, innovative, and stimulating allows you to grow as a coach.

29

GOOD PLAYERS GET BORED

As coaches, we often get upset when a gifted athlete seems to go through the basic drills in what appears to be a halfhearted way. We may feel he is being disrespectful to us, to the team, and to the game. There probably is some truth to that, but if we stop to think about it and put ourselves in the athlete's shoes, we may have a better understanding of how he feels and how to coach him more effectively.

Talented players who are required to repeat the same drills over and over lose enthusiasm. It is unrealistic to expect an athlete to be perfect at a skill every time before he tries more advanced skills. We do not demand that a basketball player make every free throw before he is allowed to attempt three-pointers. In the academic world, math teachers do not demand that students correctly complete every question on a Calculus 1 test before they are allowed to take Calculus 2. Coaches and teachers alike just want to ensure that their players and students have a solid foundation before they continue to a more advanced level.

Jerry Wainwright, basketball coach at DePaul University, once told me something that made a lot of sense: "Good players get bored." In general, the more talented an athlete is, the more challenges he needs to reach his full potential. Coaches need to understand that and create specific situations to challenge and improve the gifted athlete.

The guidelines below will help facilitate that effort.

- Give the athlete a new skill or activity on a frequent basis. Sometimes you can use a new drill to work on the same skill. Most athletes, not just those who are gifted, like a change in the drills.
- Show them how the skill and activity can make them better. The gifted athlete wants to know how the skill will improve his performance. Give the athlete some examples: Michael Jordan, a slashing high-flying driver to the basket, developed his jump shot, then his three-point shot, and became a more complete and better player.
- Challenge the gifted athlete. Help him set high standards and goals. Hold him accountable for his goals. Dare him to be the best on the team, in the county, state, and country.
- Once you get through the initial teaching stages, make practice as competitive as you can. Challenge the athlete to see if he can put his skills to work when it counts. By making things competitive, you ensure the good player keeps his edge and focus.
- Help the athlete see in what way the basic skills are helpful in developing more advanced skills. My daughter Amy, a college professor, tells me that every now and then she needs to have her students spend a lesson or two refreshing skills from previous introductory classes so they can do the more advanced work. The same is true in athletics. Quarterbacks need refresher work on the footwork involved in drop steps prior to the pass. Poor footwork often leads to a poor pass.
- Continue to coach them. Often gifted athletes appear not to need or want coaching. Usually, neither is true. In fact, the gifted athlete benefits more and develops quicker than the average athlete from constructive coaching. A

coach does a player a disservice by using his talent but not pushing him to be better.

Many times, it is more difficult to get a good player to buy into your coaching than it is an average or below-average player. The gifted player wants to know the "why," as well as the "how." Great coaches do not allow talented players to simply use their talents; they challenge them to develop new talents and refine the ones they have.

30

COACHING THE LESS PASSIONATE PLAYERS

It is relatively easy and quite enjoyable to coach players who share our passion, desire, and love of the game. As coaches, we especially appreciate the kid who hangs onto our every word, the kid who wants to stay after practice for extra help, and lives and breathes the game. Not all players we coach fit that description. In fact, since most do not, we must determine how best to work with those less passionate athletes.

Before you can explore that challenge, however, you must consider some key variables in the equation: your own motivation for coaching and your athlete's motivation for participating. The motivation of a coach determines, in large part, the manner in which he coaches and what he brings to the job. Those motivating factors are numerous and, usually, fall under one or more of these descriptions.

- Athletics is what coaches know and where they achieved their strokes; they do not want to lose that.
- They like the adrenaline rush they get, mainly from the game.
- They truly love the game and want to teach others to love it.
- They enjoy the competition.

- They like being in charge.

The same is true of athletes. Usually, they are involved in athletics for one or more reasons, any one or a combination of which determines what they bring to and how they play the game.

- They are good at it.
- They like being around their friends (truer for high school athletes than college athletes).
- They like the recognition and scholarships athletics affords them.
- They like being part of something, the team.
- They enjoy competition.
- They have a passion for the game itself.

Another variable that impacts coach and athlete performance is the appreciation each has for the game. As coaches who were athletes, we tend to enjoy coaching players who approach and play the game similar to the way we did it as players. If you as a basketball coach were a fierce rebounder when you played, you especially appreciate that skill and the player who exhibits it more than a coach who was a shooter. If you were an intense defensive player, you may find it more difficult to coach a player who is not intense. By understanding and accepting the fact we will not have a lot of players on our teams who approach and play the game as we do, we can be more effective in coaching.

Generally, coaches take the game more seriously than athletes. Losing hurts more over the long run. That is understandable; coaching is your profession, the culmination of years of preparation and, depending on the length of your coaching tenure, years of commitment. In addition, the length of that tenure may be tenuous, often dependent on wins and losses. Coaches have more at stake.

Most athletes, on the other hand, do not expect to play organized sports much beyond the level at which you coach. Yes, there will be those high school athletes who are good enough to move on to junior college or college sports, but for most of your athletes, graduation will end their organized sports careers. Even fewer college athletes move into the semiprofessional or professional ranks. The majority of players, then, view their athletic careers as limited, and the degree of passion they bring to those careers may be limited as well. Look, for example, at your former high school or college teammates. I suspect that most of them are not so actively involved in the game today as you are. That is not to say they didn't love the game when they played the game. They simply made other career choices. Most of the players you have on your team today resemble those former teammates. Keeping that in mind will help you approach your players more effectively.

You can minimize the negatives of working with those players who exhibit less enthusiasm than you do toward your sport. It will take some effort on your part.

- Understanding that an athlete may be less passionate about the game and have less drive than you do may stimulate you to find out what motivates him. You can use that motivation to inspire. Trying to force an athlete to care as much as you care will frustrate both you and the athlete.
- Accepting that there is a disparity between your passion and the passion of some of your players can relieve you of trying to change them and allow you to look for different motivational approaches to encourage their enthusiasm for the game.
- Creating an environment and atmosphere that allows each player to feel he is a part of the program improves attitudes. As attitudes improve, passion increases.
- Finding your "passion" guys, those few people who generate excitement, and actively involving them in practice will result in several positive outcomes: The less passionate players will be more inclined to jump on board; the gap between your passion and your team's passion will diminish; you will appreciate your team more.
- By showing your love and passion for the game, your energy and enthusiasm will ooze over to the players.
- By recruiting passionate players, you have fostered an atmosphere designed to promote passion.

Whenever we coach a sport we are passionate about, it can be very frustrating and discouraging when others do not share our passion.

> **Remember:**
> 1. Not everybody shares your passion, nor should they have to.
> 2. You can create an environment to increase their passion
> 3. Other people's lack of passion need not dampen yours.

OVERTIME:

THE MENTAL SIDE OF COACHING

31

PLAN/PROCESS OR GOALS/ RESULTS

One of the hardest lessons to learn in golf is to focus on the plan/ process rather than on the goal/result. Staying in the moment and not looking ahead is vital to being successful on the golf course. What club do you hit? Where do you want to hit it? What kind of shot do you want to hit? You need a plan for each and every shot. Golf, probably more than any other sport, requires focus and concentration. But all sports require you to have a plan/process if you want to successfully reach your goals.

I asked a talented college basketball player what his plan was when he went entered a game. His reply was to "get a double-double," meaning 10 or more rebounds and points. When I asked him how he was going to do that, he said, "I don't know—I guess play hard." He had a goal, not a plan. Most athletes and coaches have goals; they may not even be particularly realistic, but they have been taught how important goals are to building success. Very few, however, have plans.

There is nothing wrong with goal-setting; in fact, it can help motivate us. But we need a plan or process to accomplish what we set out to do. A well thought-out, organized plan is crucial. Not having that plan allows people to get distracted, lose interest, and get discouraged.

Obviously, before we can develop our plan, we need to select our goals. In athletics, coaches and athletes usually aim high in goal-setting. Winning the conference championship, winning the state or national championship, being all-conference, all-state, and all-American are examples of lofty goal-setting. They may be reasonable goals, but they are difficult to plan for. It would be helpful to establish subgoals to help support the broader goals and provide concrete, measurable objectives that enhance focus. I believe for a coach or an athlete to meet his goals, it is important not to have too many. Two to three goals, with subgoals to support them, is ideal. Subgoals are more concrete than goals, and plans can be developed to achieve them.

Examples of team goals and subgoals are:

A. Football goal: Be the best offensive team in the league,
    - Football subgoal: Average x number of yards on first down.
    - Plan: In football, we can concentrate on a number of solid plays we believe will be good on first down. We can put emphasis on practicing these plays. We can instill in our players the importance of first downs by practicing just that. We can put emphasis on the importance of no penalties on first down. We can emphasize to our running backs the importance of making positive yards on first down, of not taking losses, instead of always trying to make the great play.
B. Basketball goal: Lead the league in scoring.
    - Basketball subgoal: Shoot x percent from the free throw line.
    - Plan: In basketball, to shoot a high free throw percentage, you can work with players that need help with technique, spend extra time on free throws, and shoot free throws competitively in practice.

Sample goals, subgoals, and plans for athletes in various sports:

Golf

Goal: Lower handicap two-three shots.

- Subgoal: Make more birdies.
- Plan: Be more aggressive shooting at the pins; make sure putts get to the hole. Develop a system whereby you can monitor and track whether you are following the plan.
- Subgoal: Maintain patience, achieve better anger management.
- Plan: Practice and focus on patience and anger management before and during a round. Read books on anger management; see a sports psychologist.

Basketball

Goal: Achieve All-Conference selection.
- Subgoal: Increase scoring average.
- Plan: Get more offensive rebounds and put backs, and fast break opportunities. Make rebounding and running the floor a priority at practice. Let a coach know of your plan and ask for help in holding you accountable. Keep track of offensive rebound attempts and fast break running attempts.

Football

Goal: Be a starting linebacker.
- Subgoal: Become a better tackler.
- Plan: Work on balance; work on better understanding of angles to the ball. Notify the linebacker coach of the plan and work with him. Keep track of your success in those areas.

An athlete will probably need help from a coach in selecting a goal and, most definitely, in developing a plan.

A couple of years ago, I caddied for Doug LaBelle, a professional golfer on the PGA tour. At that time, Doug was on the Nationwide tour, working his way up to the Big Tour. I observed Doug and other members of his pairing, as to how they approached the game during the round. It seemed to me, while other players seemed to lose their focus, concentration, and game plan, Doug never did, regardless of how he was playing. When I asked him about that later, he said, "I never want to waste a shot. One shot may be the difference in making the cut, finishing in the top ten, winning, or finishing second." He went on to explain what he meant: He did not want to hit a shot that did not work out because he did not check the yardage or the wind correctly. He did not want to miss a putt because he did not read the putt as much as he should have, or because he just got tired mentally and did not focus. He then said, "Of course, I want to shoot a low number, but if I think about that, I forget to concentrate on my plan, which is to stay totally in the moment, one shot at a time. The score will take care of itself." He has goals and subgoals, but he also has a well thought-out plan.

Once you have established your goal and your subgoals, most of your time and thought processes should be given to the plan. Concentrate on the daily duties and responsibilities and your chances of achieving your goals will be greatly enhanced.

32

THE 25 PERCENT RULE

We are what we are. Our genes and our upbringing combine to create the person we've become. We have our own style of perceiving and interacting with the world, and we've developed coping skills to enable us to live in it—attributes that make us who we are.

As coaches, we sometimes overlook the uniqueness of each individual. We try to make athletes someone we want them to be, someone other than who they are, and we become frustrated, if not outright angry, when they fail to live up to our expectations. We need to understand that it is foolish and counterproductive to try and overhaul our athletes' personalities (on or off the playing field). I believe, however, that we can adjust, and we can help our players adjust. I call that adjustment the 25 percent rule.

The 25 percent refers to the range of adjustment I believe we all have the capacity to make without entering some form of behavioral therapy. The 25 percent rule requires a willingness to extend our comfort zone, to risk trying something new to enhance the natural abilities we already have.

How does that rule apply to sports? Let's say you have a great spot-up shooter, he can really shoot and is a huge threat beyond the three-point line. That is his strength as a player, and he should not forget that. However, if that's all he can do, a smart opponent will adjust and take that strength away from him. However, if he is willing to extend his comfort zone, take a one-two-dribble pull up off a fake, not only has he added a new move but his original strength becomes even stronger. His dribble move will probably never be as good as his spot-up, but with a willingness to extend his athletic skill 25 percent, he has become a bigger threat.

That same kind of adjustment with regard to a player's personality can enhance his performance. Say you have an athlete who is fiery and intense. That is who he is. Don't try to take that away from him. To ask him to become reserved, calm, and patient is unrealistic. What is realistic, however, is to increase his focus and channel his intensity in a controlled manner that benefits him and the team. You are working to modify that behavior to an extent, thereby making him even stronger.

Unless coaches and athletes are aware of their behavioral and personal strengths and the means by which they can capitalize on them, they will be inclined to cling to that which is familiar, limiting their productivity. When we are stressed or are facing a crisis, we fall back on familiar behavior. A three-point shooter will take longer three-point shots under pressure. An intense, emotional player will become more intense and emotional. Now their strengths have become weaknesses.

The following charts will help both athletes and coaches identify their strengths and weaknesses and suggest the 25 percent directional move that might be made to enhance those strengths. The first skills chart is designed for basketball players, but a coach can substitute appropriate skills specific to other sports using the same format. The second chart focuses on the athlete's personality and is appropriate for all sports. The third and fourth charts focus on coaches and are appropriate for all sports.

Player Skills Chart

As a basketball player, you have strengths and weaknesses. If you want to be the most effective player possible, you must play to your strengths and minimize or improve your weaknesses. Before you can do that you need to take an honest look at you game.

Evaluate your game in the following areas. Be mindful of the position you play as you rate yourself. Please be completely honest. Do not give the answers that you think the coaching staff wants to see. Taking an honest inventory of yourself and your game is the first step toward improvement. Rate yourself in each category on a scale of 1 to 5 (1 = lowest, 5 = highest).

This particular player scores very high in the skill/finesse areas of shooting and passing. He scores much lower in the dirty-work areas of rebounding, defense, and aggressiveness.

Rating

- Passer   4
- Shooter   5
- Ball handler   5
- Creativity   2
- 1-on-1 ability   4
- Fast break ability   4
- Quickness   4
- Posting up   2
- Offensive rebounding   3
- Defensive rebounding   3
- Free throw shooting   5
- Running half court offense   5
- Screening   1
- Defense: on the ball   3
- Defense: off the ball   2
- Basketball IQ   5
- Three-point shooting   5
- Playing without the ball   2
- Feeding the post   5
- Shot blocking   2

A good plan for this athlete would be to understand he is skilled—and to use those skills. He would also benefit by getting out of his comfort zone (25 percent) and getting more assertive in the physically tough part of the game.

Player Personality Chart

Evaluate your personality as you view yourself. Be mindful of the character traits that emerge when you compete in the athletic arena. Rate yourself in each category on a scale of 1 to 5 (1 = lowest, 5 = highest).

This particular athlete scores high in areas of being a good teammate and lower in areas of assertiveness and toughness.

Rating

- Follower   5
- Leader   2
- Outgoing   2
- Cautious   5
- Daring   2
- Self-discipline   5
- Tolerance   5
- Vocal   2
- Positive   5
- Emotional   3
- Self-motivated   4
- Toughness   2
- Quiet   5
- Intensity   3
- Enjoy being on the team   3
- Relentlessness   2
- Easily discouraged   3
- Importance of basketball   5
- Importance of winning   5
- Confidence   2

A good plan for him would be to continue being that positive teammate but adjust his comfort zone (25 percent) in the areas of assertiveness (outgoing, talkative, emotional approach to the game).

We coaches can also benefit by assessing our coaching styles and coaching personalities.

Coaching Style Chart

Evaluate your coaching style in the following areas. Be mindful of the role you have in coaching and the position you may coach. Please be completely honest. Rate yourself in each category on a scale of 1 to 5 (1 = lowest, 5 = highest).

This coach appears to have an excellent understanding of the game. He prepares well and is good with details and the public. He would be a better coach if he would improve (25 percent) his relationships with players, on-the-floor coaching, and recruiting.

Rating

• Practice coaching	3
• Game coaching	5
• Coaching individual workouts	3
• Scouting	5
• Game preparation	5
• Recruiting	2
• Evaluation	5
• Player-coach relationships	3
• Relationships with other coaches on staff	3
• Summer camps	2
• Academics	5
• Public relations	5
• Feel for the game	5
• Proactivity	3
• Hiring and firing staff	n/a
• Office management	5
• Scheduling	5

Coaching Personality Chart

Examine your personality, how you view yourself. Be mindful of the character traits that emerge as you compete in the coaching arena. Rate yourself in each category on a scale of 1 to 5 (1 = lowest, 5 = highest).

This particular coach is a confident, strong-willed, aggressive, in-your-face type of person. He would benefit by moving 25 percent in the direction of being quieter, more tolerant, and more understanding.

Rating

- Love of game   5
- Leadership   5
- Follower   2
- Patient   2
- Intense   5
- Self-motivated   5
- Self-disciplined   3
- Sensitivity   1
- Importance of winning   5
- Willing to learn   2
- Tough   5
- Relentless   5
- Outgoing   5
- Vocal   5
- Loyal   3
- Standing up for what you believe   5
- Strong-willed   5
- Team player   2
- Confident   5
- Tolerant   1
- Quiet   1

Some questions to ask yourself as a coach:

1. Am I willing to get out of my comfort zone 25 percent?
2. Do I recognize each player's strengths personally on and off the field or floor?
3. Do I acknowledge those strengths to the athlete?
4. Do I communicate respectfully the ways in which I want each player to "extend" his play by 25 percent? Am I specific about my expectations?

33

DEVELOP MENTAL CAPACITY

To be a great athlete, requires two things: physical ability and mental capacity. The degree of physical ability an athlete has is determined by inherited traits: size, speed, height, strength, quickness, and so on, and how he makes use of those traits in developing the skills necessary for his particular sport. The same is true of mental capacity. Some athletes seem to be born with certain traits or, because of their upbringing, develop traits that are helpful in athletics, such as competitiveness, intensity, patience, and handling adversity.

If games, as many coaches say, are half mental, we coaches need to do much more to develop that part of the game. Tons of work is put into developing physical skills, but not very much work is dedicated to developing mental capacity. Because we've not been taught how to develop mental capacity, we do not know how to do it, so we do little or nothing about it.

Since so little emphasis and effort has been assigned to developing that mental capacity, the opportunity for quick and measurable success is huge.

The following is an effective four-step process to improve mental capacity.

1. Address these questions: What strengths does the athlete have in mental capacity? What does the athlete lack in

mental capacity? What is holding him back? The personality trait chart introduced in chapter 32, "The 25 Percent Rule," is a good place to start. Whatever he is lacking, and it may be several things, the first step is for the athlete to recognize that improvement is needed in these areas. That will require the athlete to look inward, which may be difficult for him to do. Probably, he will need guidance. Trust must be established and a healthy communication model put in place. With the help of a qualified and committed assistant coach, who acts as facilitator, the athlete takes an honest look at himself, seeing what strengths he has and how those strengths can be enhanced by choosing areas of mental capacity that can be developed to bring his game to another level.

2. Determine whether the athlete wants to make a change. Is he willing to make the commitment? Are there obstacles in the way that may prevent change? These concerns need to be discussed. What if a player decided he could benefit by becoming more aggressive? Maybe he thinks other players will not like him as well. If he dives on the floor for a loose ball in basketball, maybe he will be seen as showing off. Maybe he is afraid of getting hurt. All of these possibilities need to be discussed in a safe (confidential) environment, before an athlete decides, "Yes, I want to make a change."

3. After determining what areas of mental capacity the athlete wants to change (I recommend, at most, two areas to begin), what does the athlete need to do to make that happen? A plan of attack needs to be developed. For example, a golfer who has come to the conclusion he has to develop better anger management, could try the following steps:

- Visualization: practice seeing himself doing what he wants to do. See himself being calm and in control after hitting a bad shot.
- Self-talk: Talk to himself during the round about how he is going to react to a difficult situation.

- Write reminders: Place notes in strategic locations to remind himself of and reinforce the directions he wants to go.
- Practice: Use effective strategies such as deep-breathing exercises or meditation to reinforce calmness and serenity when on the course.

Another example might be a quiet, unassertive football player who wants to increase his assertiveness. He might try the following:

- Visualization: See himself standing and speaking on his own behalf.
- Self-talk: Each day before and during practice verbally affirm his goals.
- Write reminders: Place those same goals on paper and place them where he will see them repeatedly throughout the day.
- Practice: Set up a practice schedule for realizing those goals—he will speak up x number of times each day. Keep a chart to monitor progress; it will hold him accountable to himself. The chart might have the following elements:
  1. Goal: assertiveness
  2. Scale: 1 = terrible, 2 = poor, 3 = average, 4 = good, 5 = excellent
  3. Day: Monday Tuesday Wednesday Thursday Friday Saturday Sunday
- Each day the athlete charts himself, and on the days he scores a 1, 2, or 3, he writes the reason why he did not do well. He analyzes what was holding him back. He looks at his plan and checklist to see whether he has consistently been working at it.

4. Does the athlete need support? Usually, at first, he will. If so, who will provide that support? It must be someone with whom the athlete has developed a sense of trust. Often an assistant coach fills that role well because he is present at practices and games. The coach (or other person) must be fully committed to the plan and consistently work with the athlete. Together, the coach and athlete develop the means

by which the coach supports the player, whether that it is to remind him, call him out, develop a code word, or so on. The coach helps hold the athlete accountable.

If the player truly commits to the program and gets consistent support from a coach, remarkable improvement can be made. During the 2006–2007 basketball season, I worked with Bradley Strickland, a senior at Evansville University. Bradley wanted to have a more aggressive mental approach to rebounding. He developed a plan of attack to accomplish that goal. He not only used many of the techniques outlined above but also developed some of his own, such as writing the word rebound on his hands. He asked Jason Zimmerman, an assistant coach, to support him on a daily basis. His rebounding stats from his junior year to his senior year improved, and he become one of the top rebounders in the Missouri Valley Conference. He bought into the program of improving his mental capacity and found success.

34

ANALYZE YOUR GAME

I discuss ways to develop mental capacity in the previous chapter. Now let's take a look at how an athlete analyzes his game. The two activities have similarities as well as differences. Mental ability is a more long-term approach for the athlete to use and strengthen certain areas of his mental game. Analyzing your game is making adjustments after, and sometimes during the game, to better utilize your skills. Analyzing your game is a constant tweaking of the mental capacity.

One of the challenges of coaching is motivating athletes to improve their game. We question why some players are so much more successful at it than others, and we come up with any number of reasons.

- One player works harder at it than another.
- One player is receiving better instruction than another.
- One player handles adversity and pressure better than another.
- One player is more naturally skilled and talented than another.

Sometimes, though, we find such traits to be fairly equal among athletes, and still, one will improve faster than another. Why? I believe the explanation is that some players know how to study and analyze their play, helping them to develop their game more readily.

It is said that if you keep doing what you are doing, you will keep getting what you have been getting. Or to put it another way, Practice makes perfect only if you're doing it right in the first place. In other words, if what you are doing is not working, you need to make some changes or adjustments to get a different result. Most athletes, at every level, struggle to make changes and adjustments. They have been playing a certain way for years and at times have had success. But now, at a higher level of competition, that way of play is not working as well. They are less in control; the game happens to them. They do not have a consistent game plan and do not make adjustments from game to game to allow them to be more efficient. They do not, for the most part, analyze their play after a game, or if they do, they do not do it effectively.

What is it that inhibits an athlete from effectively analyzing his game?

First, I don't believe athletes are taught that skill. They begin organized play at a young age and are told (sometimes badly) what to do to become better players. The role of the player is to do what he is told. Seldom does the player learn how to figure out what does and does not work for him. In effect, he has been overcoached.

Second, some coaches do not know how to analyze a player's game. Others, for whatever reason, do not share that information with the athlete. Instead of teaching athletes how to analyze for themselves, they dispense that analysis and retain the power that having information provides.

Third, although coaching today is far more advanced, complex, and sophisticated than it was years ago, the emphasis is still placed heavily on the physical rather than the mental aspect of the game. Coaches, like players, have been trained to perform in a certain way. Usually the training emphasis is on the physical part of the game, not the mental.

So, how do we coaches help players learn better to analyze their game? Basically, to teach athletes to do the same thing coaches do; help players learn to *debrief*, that is, to sit down with film and go over the athlete's play, looking at both the positive and negative aspects of the game. It may not be difficult for the athlete to recognize the missed shots, tackles, or putts, but it is difficult to analyze the "why."

Next, the coach needs to help the player recognize what type of adjustment he needs to make to improve play. For example, to make more shots, I need consistently to use my legs and not rush my shot. Or to become a better tackler, I need to wrap up the ball carrier. Or to become a better putter, I need to hit the ball with a better pace.

In each instance, the player needs to practice that adjustment repeatedly.

Once the athlete, with the help of a coach, has identified the problem areas and kinds of adjustments that need to take place, together they will *create a plan*. What drills can be used to help develop a particular skill? What coach will be able and willing to help develop that skill? Specifics of that plan, including a timetable if appropriate, should be put into writing for accountability purposes—accountability to self—in this case, the athlete.

The goal, of course, is to model this process with the athlete until he is able to analyze his play without assistance. The debriefing process can be done at first with the help of a coach and film, but the athlete himself needs to be going over each play, positive and negative, to see what changes need to be made.

Perhaps the best example of an athlete who was good at analyzing his game was Michael Jordan. Whenever Jordan had a poor game, he almost always came back the next game with an outstanding effort. Sure, he probably was more determined and focused than the average player, but he also made adjustments; he figured out what he was doing poorly and worked to correct that.

Once an athlete understands he has the ability to adjust and correct from game to game and sometimes even during the game, he becomes empowered and will see dramatically positive results.

Play Improvement Plan

I. Debrief
  A. Analyze play
  B. Determine needed adjustments
II. Create plan
  A. Select skill drills
  B. Request coaching assistance
  C. Practice

35

HOW DO YOU WANT TO BE COACHED?

One of the keys to being an effective coach is getting athletes to buy into what the coach is selling. An athlete needs to believe in the coach; when he does, his coachability improves, and consequently, his development improves. With that in mind, a coach must determine the best way to attract his players.

The idea of "attracting" players may offend some coaches, especially those who have been at it for quite a while. Their attitude is, "This is the way I coach, and I'm too old to change. It is up to the player to adjust to me." That may be the simplest and easiest way for the coach to do things, but is it the most effective? If our goal is to develop the athlete the best we can, then there may be more effective ways to reach him.

Studies show that people learn and respond differently to different styles of teaching. If, as coaches, we find what style fits an individual, we have a better chance of being effective in teaching him. That does not mean we have to change the coach we are. We coach in a way that fits our personalities, but we can make adjustments.

During conversations with coaches, I frequently hear them make statements about what motivates a player. "This kid constantly needs to be chewed out." Or "This kid needs frequent pats on the back." They may not always be right in their assessment, but they are trying to figure out the best way to motivate the player. In effect, they function as psychologists and behavioral evaluators. When they are inaccurate, they make the situation worse. The athlete struggles with the coach and with the game.

How, then, as a coach, do you know what is the best and most effective way to get an athlete to respond to your coaching? What will inspire him? Some coaches use personality profiles, which if used correctly, can be helpful. However, personality profiles can be time consuming and complicated.

How about asking the athlete? If you sincerely want an answer, you may get information that will help develop the player, personally and athletically, and thus help the team as well. When asking an athlete how he would like to be coached, it is important to communicate clearly with the athlete a couple of things:

- As coach, I really want to know. Be honest with me; do not tell me what you think I want to hear.
- Don't take the easy route. I am not asking how you want to be coached so it will be nice for you, but rather what style is best for you to come as close as possible to your potential.

Asking a player how he wants to be coached does not necessarily mean that will be the only way he will be coached. Coaches will have a style of coaching the entire team, but at times they may use a different style of coaching—one more suited to an individual player.

If a coach chooses to talk with players about what coaching styles are most effective for them, he might look at some of the following questions to obtain information:

1. Is one-on-one coaching effective with you?
2. Do demonstrations help you? (Some kids are visual learners; they need to see it.)
3. Do you respond to verbal directions?
4. Are you sensitive in the athletic arena?
5. Does being praised motivate you as an athlete?
6. Are you self-motivated as an athlete?

7. Are you self-disciplined as an athlete?
8. Do you think you benefit much from film work?
9. Is having close relationships with the coaches helpful to you as a player?
10. How do you handle confrontation from a coach?

When asking these types of questions of players, the coach could ask the player to put himself on a continuum from one to ten. By doing this, the coach can obtain insight about the player. For example, if a player says he does not handle confrontation from a coach very well, you can let him say what would, in his opinion, be the most effective manner for the coach to confront him. Not every question will need a lot of analysis, but the ones that do can be discussed, helping the coach get a better understanding of the player. Also, I think the responses to this interaction can serve as common ground for the coach to tell the player how he coaches, disciplines, confronts, and so on, so the player can anticipate that in advance and, perhaps, not take that behavior personally. If the conversation takes place between the athlete and an assistant coach, the assistant can tell the athlete how the head coach coaches to the same end.

By no means am I suggesting a coach go soft on a kid or fail to address his mistakes and shortcomings. I am suggesting that the best way to do that is to clarify the means by which that will happen most effectively. Additionally, the coach and athlete start to develop a relationship and partnership

I have heard athletes say after they finish their career that their coach held them back and did not understand them. I realize often times that is sour grapes, the athlete was not as talented as he thought he was, or did not apply himself, but often I believe there is some truth to the statement. How sad if that is true. As coaches, we want to enhance the career of the athlete, not hinder it. I believe we have a responsibility to examine new and different ways to make sure we are coaching the athlete in a way to let him play as close to his potential as possible. So what is wrong with letting the athlete have some input into what he believes is the most effective way for him to be coached?

36

USE DATA TO GET PLAYERS TO BUY IN

The *game* in athletics has been usurped. No longer a simple contest between two teams and coaching staffs, it plays out before, during, and after the actual contest when others "weigh in" on the event. The actual contest and every play, real or anticipated, is predicted, highlighted, and analyzed by sportscasters, odds makers, and armchair quarterbacks. That game-outside-the-game becomes the real event, enabling everyone the opportunity to play.

Often during a football or basketball game, you will hear an announcer say there is not much a team can do to stop the other team. Or when a running back is racking up the yards or a basketball player is on his way to a 40-point game, the announcer will say there is not much the other team can do to stop him. The announcer is "weighing in" on the contest, making a prediction, which either will or will not be borne out by the game's result.

You hear similar predictions from others: One team is rated in the top 10; another is not rated at all. One team is a 30-point favorite. One player is rated over another. In each case, a prediction is being made regarding the likely success of the team or player. Predicting success has become a game itself.

The attention and support this game-outside-the-game brings to athletics is a two-edged sword that is beyond the scope of this book. It is the impact that it can have on the actual contest that needs to be addressed here.

Young players, easily distracted by the hype that surrounds athletics, too often buy into the opinions of others, whether those opinions have merit or not. To fall victim to the mentality that there is not much you can do when playing against a great team or player creates a giving-in mind-set that compromises the possibility of winning. Keeping athletes focused and positive is an integral part of the coach's responsibility.

The realization that, despite the odds, players and coaches have the ability to control their fate was exhibited to me several years ago when I had the opportunity to watch a friend and former player of mine, Dan Majerle, and the Phoenix Suns play against Michael Jordan and the Chicago Bulls. Jordan, guarded by Dan, had an outstanding game.

After the game, I commented to Dan that Jordan got a roll and when that happens, it is almost impossible to stop him. His reply, quite emphatically, was that it wasn't what Jordan did, but rather what he, Dan, did not do that enabled Jordan's play. He told me that when he watches tape of the game, he is certain to see what mistakes he made that allowed Jordan to score so many points. Since that conversation, I understand how important having accurate information, the kind that Dan gleaned from watching game films, is in preparing for your opponent.

A coach must determine, like Dan did, which part of the play is controlled by the opponent and which part is controlled by his own team. I think he will be surprised to find that a large percentage of the time, that control rests with him. Of course, mistakes will happen. There will be missed tackles and fumbles in football, turnovers in basketball, and double faults in tennis, but if the coach has good information and if his team performs to standard, he will be successful in empowering his players, helping them to understand that they are capable of winning.

Data that distinguishes who controls the game or play best provides a coach and team the power needed to make better decisions. Examples of this kind of data to collect by sport include:

- *Tennis.* How many points did my opponent earn (great serve, great return) versus a poor shot decision by us?
- *Soccer.* How many goals did our opponent score because of their great passes, strategy, and skill versus poor defensive play by us?
- *Baseball.* How many hits did the other team get because of great batting versus our poor pitch selection or ball placement?
- *Football.* How many yards did the opponent earn because of great execution or deception versus our poor tackling and angle pursuit?

During one three-year period as a consultant, I charted the defensive play of more than thirty college basketball games. By looking at the film after the game, I wanted to find whether the baskets made by the opponents were earned or the result of defensive mistakes. I was amazed by the results: Over thirty games, opponents "earned" an average of 25 percent of scored points, leaving a lot of room for defensive improvement. Since the rating is somewhat subjective, it is important for a team to have the same person or team of people do the evaluation from game to game.

The following table evaluates eight basketball players, using defensive mistakes to determine earned and unearned points: *Jeremy* = A; *Jake* = B; *Chet* = C; *Jeff* = D; *Hank* = E; *Jason* = F; *Evan* = G; *Nathan* = H.

Defensive mistake	A	B	C	D	E	F	G	H	Opponent's unearned points
Control of dribbler	3		2	8	3	1		5	22
Offensive rebounds		3		2					5
Fouls		2		1				2	5
Poor rotation		2	1						3
Defensive transition	2			4	2				8
Low post defense	2		2					2	6
Communication	1			3	1				5
Contesting shots					5		1		6
Opponent's unearned points	8	7	5	18	11	1	1	9	60
Opponent's earned points									20
Opponent's total points									80

145

Sometimes the cause of unearned points can be divided between two areas, such as not controlling the dribbler and poor rotation. Sometimes, too, the cause of the breakdown enabling unearned points can be divided between two players, one player for not controlling the dribbler and another having poor rotation.

We coaches and players can learn a great deal from good data:

- We control our destiny. If, as in the table above, only 25 percent of the 80 points are opponent-earned, by reducing our weaknesses we can improve dramatically.
- We can find out what aspect of our defense is hurting us. In the sample game, the table shows that not controlling the dribbler was a big factor in the game. That can change from game to game depending on the style of play of the other team. But we know we need to work at containing the dribbler better.
- We can find out what players are hurting us defensively. In this case Jeff was responsible for giving up 18 points. Collecting this kind of data helps hold players accountable.

Whatever sport you coach, the advantages of charting your team's play are numerous. The data will show that it is not so much what your opponent is doing as it is what you are doing or not doing that determines success. I have seen firsthand how Tod Kowalczyk, the head coach of the Wisconsin-Green Bay Phoenix, uses data to get his players to buy into whatever concept or idea he is stressing. Using data can be a helpful tool.

EPILOGUE:

ADDITIONAL THOUGHTS

Examine Yourself as a Coach

- *Do you practice sportsmanlike conduct?* I believe as coaches we have a responsibility to demonstrate good sportsmanship. Athletic competition and the pursuit of winning can be stressful, but that does not excuse our being unsportsmanlike. Too often, after a tough, hard-fought game, we see coaches give a halfhearted handshake and not say a word to each other. What is wrong with saying "congratulations" or "good game"? Sadly, players often demonstrate better sportsmanship during and after the game than the coaches. Coaches should set the standard for players and fans to follow.

- *Do you try to foresee the future?* Avoid beginning the season by looking ahead at the schedule and predicting your team's wins and losses. When we look ahead, we fall into the trap of taking teams too lightly and give ourselves an out by anticipating which teams will give us difficulty. How can we coaches know, before the season begins, how other teams will perform?

- *Do you know your limitations?* Coaches will face any number of issues for which they are ill prepared. Depression, ADD, mental illness, and drug and alcohol problems are just a few of the issues that your athletes, perhaps even members of the staff, bring to the program. You are neither trained nor licensed to handle these situations. Identify appropriate resources so you can make referrals as necessary. Be prepared to support the professional's recommendations.

- *Do you make snap judgments?* Don't make up your mind about a player's ability too quickly. It is easy to watch a player in your program, high school or college, and quickly come to the conclusion that he can or cannot play. When we do that, we see and evaluate the player with a biased eye. The player who we determine *can* play may get a pass when he plays poorly. We tend to be overly critical of a player we determine cannot help the team. I've been wrong about a player several times, and

I suspect other coaches have been guilty of that as well. Kids develop and mature at different rates. Remember: If an athlete is in your program, it is your responsibility to believe in and work with him.

The same principle applies to recruiting:

- *Do not judge too quickly.* My good friend Dave Telep, of Scout.com, likes to see a basketball player play five times. Of course, that is not always possible. But at the very minimum, if a player comes highly recommended, you should see him play three times. You will find there is a high, low, and medium performance. It is a simple standard to adhere to. Do your homework. Call an opposing coach. Ask about the kid, his intelligence, discipline, desire, and so on. As an assistant coach, don't let the head coach see him once, have a bad game, and dump him. If you like him, make your case. It is your job to get the best players. Do not let a good one slip away.

- *Evaluate the evidence that you see.* Is he succeeding? The answer should not be yes, he is succeeding now, but when we play an opponent who is bigger and stronger, he may not be as good. If the player is performing well in practice, give him an opportunity in the game. I had a young man on my high school team several years ago by the name of Tom Jones. He was a six-foot guard who played very little as a junior. The team that year was very good, and even though he looked good in practice, I did not give him much opportunity to play in games. I did that, in part, because I did not want to change the lineup and risk jeopardizing the success we were having, but, mostly, it was because I was convinced that the way he played would not work against good athletes and teams. He was not big, strong, fast, or quick, but he was crafty. The next year he started, averaged 25 points a game, and made first team all-state. At the time, I did no appreciate crafty. I do now.

Examine Yourself as a Person

- *Are you humble?* The coaching world today seems to have some coaches with big egos and a sense of self-importance. A healthy ego is needed to be successful in any profession, especially coaching, but it should be balanced with some humility. Dale Race, former assistant basketball coach at Wisconsin-Green Bay, is an example of a person with a healthy amount of humility. During the 2007–2008 basketball season, Coach Race coached in his one thousandth college game, some as an assistant, many as a head coach. He has been elected as a coach or player to five halls of fame, but talking with him you would never suspect it. He is quietly proud of his achievements but humble and appreciative of all those who have helped him along the way.

- *Do you demonstrate unconditional love?* I attended a funeral where a lady gave a eulogy for her mother. The lady, who had had some troubled and difficult times, talked about how her mother was always there for her. "My mother let me know that, at times, she did not approve of my behavior, but she always supported and believed in me—especially, when times were the toughest." Too often, coaches are supportive of players when they are doing well, but when things are not going well, they withhold their love and support. The player needs the support and love most when he goes from a starter to a sub, when he is struggling academically, when he is not playing well. To ignore a player, to be unsupportive or distant at those moments is not demonstrating unconditional love.

- *Do you live by the golden rule?* Show some consideration toward opposing coaches. Too often animosity rears its ugly head between rival coaches. Yes, you are competing and sometimes recruiting against this person. And you may not respect how he conducts business, but he is in the same profession and dealing with many of the same issues as you are. Do not add to the strain that already exists in the profession. Remember, too, the visibility that comes with coaching. Your behavior does not go unnoticed.

- *Do you strive to achieve "good chemistry"?* Every year I hear coaches lament about how their team this year does not have good chemistry. Guess what. Chemistry does not just happen. A number of topics discussed in this book can help you achieve good chemistry. If everybody in the program models healthy behavior, the odds of the chemistry on the team being good are greatly enhanced.

- *Do you treat everyone with respect?* Everyone is worthy of respect. When I observe coaches, I am interested in how they interact with people lower on the pecking order. In colleges, it is not how the coach deals with the university president or the athletic director, but rather with the walk-on and the student manager. In high school it is not how the coach deals with the superintendent, the principal, or the athletic director but rather how he treats the last man on the bench, the team manager, and the custodian. Does he treat them with respect and kindness? A person's true character is revealed in his interactions with people who have less power than he does.

- *Are you courageous?* There will be opportunities in your coaching career to demonstrate courage, such as dealing with illness, your own or someone else's; standing up for what you believe in, regardless of the consequences; or doing what is right, no matter how difficult. When I think of coaches who have shown great courage, I think of Kay Yow, the coach of North Carolina State's women's basketball team. Coach Yow has battled cancer for several years and has become an inspiration to many other cancer survivors because of her determination in fighting the disease. I also think of my friend Trey Schwab, a former assistant basketball coach at Marquette University. Trey contracted a rare lung disease, which he fought for two years without complaining or feeling sorry for himself, before he received a lung transplant in February 2004.

I remember self-reporting an ineligible player on my team. He happened to be the star player on the team, which at the time was rated number 1 in the state. While examining his transcript, I discovered it had been inaccurately interpreted when he transferred from another school. He was in his fifth year of high school and thus ineligible to compete. I made the decision to report it to the principal, knowing the inaccuracy probably would never have been discovered, and that our chances for a state championship would be greatly reduced. It was the right thing to do, even if it proved to be difficult for the young man, the team, and me. As coaches, we are teaching life lessons to young people, and when an opportunity to exhibit courage appears, we need to grasp it.

Put Your People Skills to Work in Coaching

Help athletes channel, not stifle, their competitive enthusiasm. Have you ever noticed that the person who sits back, does not tip his hand, and prefers to go unnoticed is seldom criticized? The person who speaks up is vulnerable to criticism. The same dynamic is true in athletics. The athlete or coach who is unafraid to show or say how he feels is subjected to analysis and criticism. In our athletes, we see some of that assertiveness revealed in what we perceive to be inappropriate behavior: yelling at teammates, getting technical fouls, and so on. The athlete who cares pours his heart into his event and, sometimes, goes too far. Of course, we must address inappropriate behavior; too frequently, however, we stifle the competitive spirit in the process.

Mark Johnson, a friend of mine who is now a country club golf professional, was, as a kid, a talented golfer with a bad temper. His parents warned him that if he continued to behave inappropriately, he would no longer be allowed to play golf. He did a complete 180-degree turn, refusing to allow himself to get upset or angry. In the process, he lost his competitive drive. Looking back, he regrets giving up on his goal of becoming a great golfer. His parents, who simply wanted to correct his poor behavior, helped stifle his competitiveness. As coaches, we need to recognize a competitive spirit and help channel that energy appropriately.

Examine Coaching Styles, Techniques, and Ideas

- *Make opponents do what they are not inclined to do.* Make a fast break team slow down. Make a passing team, run; double the great receiver, and see if the other receiver can beat you. When you make teams get out of their comfort zone, when you make athletes try to do something they normally do not do, there is usually a struggle.

- *Be creative in planning off-season programs.* Since college and high school coaches do not have the opportunity to work with their athletes on a year-round basis, creating an effective workout program is important. Young people sometimes think it is the amount of time they put into practice that is key. You need to help them understand that it is how they use that practice time that is key.

- *Avoid overcoaching and undercoaching.* Overcoaching is when the team is given too much information, preparation is extreme, and the coach is trying to coach every play. Undercoaching is when the team is not given enough information, preparation is limited, and the coach seldom tries to control the game. It seems to me there is a proper amount of preparation and coaching that needs to go into a game, which can change from team to team and from game to game. Finding that medium is of utmost importance. On the whole, however, I believe more games are lost because of overcoaching than undercoaching. Somehow the coach does not feel quite as bad if the team loses when he tried to prepare the team for every possible situation that could arise. But all that information and preparation may actually have contributed to the loss, because it inhibited the athletes' ability to play free and relaxed.

- *Make practice realistic.* Several years ago I was in the locker-room of Marquette University after they had

154

beaten UNC Charlotte in a close game. While the players were showering and getting dressed, one player, Steve Novak, now playing in the NBA, was still in uniform and pacing back and forth. When I asked him if he was okay, he replied, "I can't believe I missed that free throw; it could have cost us the game. I wish I could go out there and shoot free throws right now." "OK," I said, "let's go." When we got out to the arena, we went to the same basket at which Steve had missed the free throw in the last ten seconds of the game. Just before Steve got to the free throw line, I informed him that he had one free throw. If he made it, he got the bonus, if not, back to the locker room. He made both free throws. We made the free throw session as much like game conditions as possible.

- *Trust your instincts.* Many years ago the high school team I was coaching was playing our archrival in a game that might well have determined the league champion. The game was very tight, and we were down one point, with two seconds to go in the game, when my best player, Chip Pisoni, was fouled in the act of shooting. I called time-out, in effect icing my own player at the free throw line. I was criticized for calling time-out by a number of people, but I knew Chip well enough to know that if he missed the free throw, it would be because he was fatigued not because he was nervous or pressured. He made both free throws and we won the game. What I did was out of the norm, but I trusted my instincts.

- *Play every play.* This is an expression we hear more and more often from coaches. Tyler Hansbrough, of the University of North Carolina, is described as a player who plays every play, who doesn't take plays off. Golfers are an excellent example of athletes who cannot afford to take a play (shot) off if they want to be successful. That being said, why do so many players not play every play? A contributing factor is that they do not know how or do not practice it. As coaches we spend a lot of time talking

155

about playing every play, but we do not give our athletes ways to learn how to do that. I believe a good place to start is to try and play every play for a shorter segment: three or four possessions in basketball, one game of tennis, or three straight minutes in soccer. By doing that, the athlete has a better chance to grasp the concept and get the feel of the process. The next step is to extend the length of playing every play until it is done the entire game.

- *Adapt the teaching style to the lesson.* Be demanding when teaching effort-related activities, like rebounding and defense in basketball, running out fly balls in baseball, and hustling to get to balls in tennis. Be calmer and more patient when teaching skilled, decision-related activities, such as passing against a zone defense in basketball, calling an audible in football, and passing the baton in relays. Some things can be accomplished through sheer determination and energy; others need more understanding and patience.

- *Accentuate the positive.* I once heard an interview with a great shooter whose name I do not recall. The interviewer asked him what thoughts he had when he missed six or seven shots in a row. He replied, "As good a shooter as I am, I know the next one is going in." The interviewer then asked, "What if you make six or seven shots in a row?" The shooter responded, "Then I am on a roll and I know everything is going in." Taken aback, the interviewer countered, "But you can't have it both ways." "Why not," the shooter responded, more statement than question. Why not, indeed.

- *Use 10-practice data to assess your team.* If you evaluate your practices on a scale of 1 to 10, with 1 being awful and 10 being great, I would be most interested in seeing not how many 10s you have, but rather, how few 1 through 5s. It is what you do when you do not feel good, you aren't in the zone, and things are not going your way that will determine how successful you will be—as a player and a team. Tiger Woods is excellent at that. When he does not have his swing or does not putt well, he can still turn a potential 77 into a 72. He, as they say, grinds it out. Can you motivate your team to turn a 3 practice into a 6 or 7? If you can do that on a consistent basis, then when you get behind early in the game, you will have a better chance of fighting back.

The suggestions I offer here are born of years of experience as a coach and coaching consultant and through the hard work of getting to know, like, and respect myself as a person who loves to coach. As coaches, you must find your own way to reach success, however you define it. For me, success means touching lives in a way that values and empowers each person, that creates a safe place for growth and development, and that promotes and honors the commitments and hard work of all.

The whole, it is said, is greater than the sum of its parts. In sports, every member of the program contributes to the value of that whole. And it is your responsibility and your privilege as coach to see that each part—athlete, assistant coach, support staff—makes the greatest contribution he can to the success of the whole.

49779861R00105

Made in the USA
Lexington, KY
19 February 2016